CONTENTS.

FARCES AND GARNITURES,
FISH,
BEEF,
MUTTON,
VEAL,

FARCES AND GARNITURES,

CALLED ALSO GARNISH AND GARNISHING, USED TO DECORATE OR ORNAMENT DISHES.

With Bread.—Put in a tureen about a pound of the soft part of bread, and cover with broth; when it has absorbed the broth, place it in a stewpan, set it on a slow fire, and leave till it becomes a thick paste; stir now and then, then mix well with it three yolks of eggs, and it is ready for use.

With Cabbage.—Throw into boiling water a little salt and a middling-sized cabbage; boil it half an hour, take it from the kettle with a skimmer, throw it in cold water, and drain it, pressing it a little in the drainer to force the water out; cut off the stump, and chop the cabbage fine. Have in a stewpan on the fire, three or four ounces of fresh butter; put the cabbage in when the butter is half melted, sprinkling on while stirring a teaspoonful of flour; pour on it, little by little, some broth, stirring the while, and when it has a fine brownish color, wet with broth enough to boil it; season with salt, a little grated nutmeg, and four pepper-corns; boil gently till the sauce is thick enough, take away the pepper-corns, and use.

With Combs of Chicken.—Soak the combs over night in cold water, and then clean them well by wiping roughly with a coarse towel, wetted and salted; wash and drain them; put a dozen of them in a saucepan with two sweetbreads blanched, cover the whole with broth, and boil till done; then add salt, pepper, a few drops of lemon-juice, and it is ready for use.

With Cauliflowers.—Proceed as for cabbage in every particular, except that it does not require as long doing.

With *Croutons.*—Cut pieces of soft part of stale bread in different shapes, and fry them on both sides in butter or fat.

For potage, they are cut in dice, but for decorating dishes, they are cut either round, square, oblong, or of a heart, star-like, half moon, butterfly, or flower shape, and about one-quarter of an inch thick. Take them off with a skimmer, and turn into a colander to drain.

The cut *d* is used for potage, and *a*, *b*, *c*, etc., are used to decorate.

Duxelle.—Make a *fines-herbes* sauce, and when ready to be used, add half a gill of gravy, and give one boil; add also two or three yolks of eggs, simmer one minute, and use warm.

Mushrooms, whole or in slices, may be added at the same time the yolks of eggs are added.

With Eggs.—Mash and mix well together six hard-boiled yolks of eggs with three yolks not cooked, salt and pepper. Put the mixture in parts on the paste-board, which must be previously dusted with flour; roll each part and give it the shape of a small egg (a pigeon's egg or a little larger). When the whole is thus prepared, drop in boiling water, boil till cooked, and use to decorate meat or fish.

Financière.—A garniture *financière* is the same as a garniture with combs of chicken, to which are added some mushrooms and truffles, both cut in slices.

It is generally served with a roast chicken.

With Livers.—Geese livers are the best, being the fattest. Drop two geese livers in boiling water and a little salt, boil three minutes and drain. Put in a saucepan one gill of broth, same of white wine, Sauterne or Catawba, a tablespoonful of gravy, six pepper-corns, two or three stalks of parsley, salt, and the livers; set on the fire and boil gently for about twenty-five minutes.

Take off the livers, boil a few minutes longer to thicken the sauce, turn it over the livers through a strainer, and it is ready.

The same may be done with the livers of poultry or any other kind of birds; the seasonings are the same, and the proportion is according to the size or to the number of livers.

Besides being used as garnishing, it may be served as a breakfast dish.

Macédoine.—Blanch a dozen of Brussels cabbages. Blanch also half a dozen asparagus cut in pieces about an inch long. Put four ounces of butter in a saucepan on the fire, and when melted put it into a gill of carrots, same of turnips, both cut with a vegetable spoon, also a dozen small onions; stir now and then till the whole is about half done, when add a little over a pint of broth and the Brussels cabbages; boil about ten minutes. Then add again the blanched asparagus, half a dozen mushrooms, broth just enough to cover the whole, simmer till every thing is done, salt and pepper to taste, a pinch of sugar and it is ready for use.

Water may be used instead of broth, but is inferior.

A *macédoine* may be served with any meat—roasted, baked, or broiled.

With Mushrooms.—Chop fine half a pint of fresh mushrooms and two tablespoonfuls of parsley. Set a saucepan on the fire with two ounces of fat grated salt pork in it, as much butter, and as soon as the butter is melted put the mushrooms and parsley in; season with salt, pepper, a little grated nutmeg, and a quarter of a pint of white wine; let boil gently till reduced to a jelly, and use.

When done, three or four yolks of eggs may be mixed with it.

With Onions.—Put a dozen onions in a crockery saucepan and half cover them with broth. Cover the pan as well as possible, simmer till cooked, then add a teaspoonful of sugar, salt, simmer again for about ten minutes, basting now and then, and serve warm with beef, mutton, or venison.

Quenelles.—Chop fine one pound of fresh veal, half lean and half fat—the fat nearest the kidney is the best; then pound it well and mash it through a sieve. Mix two yolks of eggs with it, and season to taste with salt, pepper, nutmeg grated, and powdered cinnamon. Spread flour on the paste-board, put a teaspoonful of meat here and there; roll gently each part into small balls, using as little flour as possible. They may also be rolled of an olive shape. Throw the balls into boiling broth or boiling water at the first boiling, boil five minutes and drain. As soon as cold they are ready for use.

Boulettes, fricadelles, godiveau, and *quenelles* are one and the same thing.

Whole eggs may be used instead of the yolks only, add also a few bread-crumbs. To the seasonings above some parsley chopped fine may be added.

Make *quenelles* with any kind of meat—butcher's meat, poultry, and game, also with fish well boned.

To the lean meat add the same weight of fat veal, as above directed, or, in its stead, beef suet.

Truffles or mushrooms, or both, may be added to the mixture, either of meat or of fish.

Quenelles are used for garnitures, etc. They may be fried instead of boiled.

Salpicon.—Cut in dice an equal quantity of each, and to weigh altogether about one pound and a half, calf sweetbreads, livers, or flesh of fowls, and ham—three kinds in all; also two mushrooms and two truffles; all must be nearly cooked in water beforehand. Put them in a stewpan, season with salt, pepper, a bay-leaf, a clove of garlic, an onion, a sprig of parsley, and one of thyme; cover with half a pint of broth, and as much of white wine; set on a slow fire; it must not boil, but simmer gently; stir now and then till the whole is well cooked; take out the bay-leaf, onion, garlic, parsley, and thyme. In case the sauce should not be thick enough, add a little fecula, stir, and leave awhile longer on the fire, and it is ready for use.

With Truffles.—Slice the truffles and put them in a saucepan with a pinch of sugar, broth and claret wine enough to cover them, half of each, simmer for about twenty minutes, add a little potato starch, boil gently till it begins to thicken, and use.

Lobster Butter.—Put the flesh of the two large claws of a boiled lobster with a little of the inside, about a tablespoonful, in a mortar and pound well. Add about the same volume of good butter and pound again till the whole is well mixed. It is then mashed through a fine sieve, and is ready for use. When the lobster has coral, it is pounded with the rest, and gives a fine color to the butter.

If the lobster has no coral, a piece of the reddest part of the shell is pounded with the rest, when the butter is to be colored.

This butter may be used instead of ordinary butter for fish-sauces, or for making a *maître d'hôtel* for boiled fish, or for garnishing the same.

To clarify it, just put the butter into a bowl when made, put the bowl in a boiling *bain-marie* for about half an hour, take off and immediately turn it through a cloth into a bowl half full of cold water. The cloth must be rather twisted, to cause the butter to run through. When it is in the bowl, stir it till rather hard; work it in a ball, and wipe it dry.

Thus clarified it is finer than when used merely mixed.

The same butter may be made, and in the same way, with *craw-fish*, *prawns*, and *shrimps*.

Horse-radish Butter.—Grate some horse-radish and mix it well with about the same volume of butter, mash through a sieve, and it is ready for use.

Tarragon and *garlic* butter are made as the above.

If the butter be found too strong, use more butter and less of garlic, etc.

Ravigote Butter (called also *Beurre de Montpellier*).—Blanch the following spices: parsley, tarragon, chives, chervil—parsley and chervil in equal proportion and about half as much of the two others, about two handfuls altogether—drain dry and put them in a mortar with two anchovies boned, one shallot chopped and bruised in a coarse towel, half a dozen capers, a rather small piece of pickled cucumber, four ounces of butter, two hard-boiled yolks of eggs, and the juice of half a lemon. Pound the whole well together, then add a tablespoonful of essence of spinach, mix well, mash through a sieve, and use.

This butter is excellent to decorate and to eat with cold fish. It is sometimes used with cold birds.

Hazel-nut Butter.—Pound some hazel-nuts or filberts and then mix throughly with good butter, mash through a sieve, and use as ordinary butter. The proportion according to taste. It is easily prepared, and is delicious.

Do the same with *pea-nuts*, or any other nut.

Melted Butter.—Put butter in a crockery vessel and place it above a pan of water or some other liquid, heated but not boiling, so that the butter will melt slowly and gradually. Sometimes the butter may be wanted soft only, or what is called melted soft, or thoroughly melted. It is easy to obtain those different states above with heated liquor, and the butter, though melted, is more firm than when melted on the fire.

Scented Butter.—Whenever a certain flavor is desired with butter, put a piece of firm and good butter in a bowl with a few drops of essence, knead well, and then mash through a sieve.

PURÉES.

Purées are made with vegetables, but when the flesh or poultry or other birds is mashed through a sieve after being cooked, it is sometimes called a *purée* also.

The bones of a ham, after the flesh is disposed of, is the most excellent thing you can put with the vegetables to boil them in order to make *purées*.

One-third of the bones of a middling-sized ham is enough for about a quart of vegetables.

When you have no ham bones, use four ounces of good salt pork, as lean as possible; but never use smoked pork, it gives a disagreeable taste to the purée.

Of Dry Beans, white or colored, Kidney, Lima, or any other kind.—Dry beans must be soaked in cold water, or even in lukewarm water, when in a hurry. According to the nature of the beans, they must be soaked for from six to twenty-four hours.

Soak a quart of beans as directed above; drain and put them in a saucepan with one-third of the bones of a ham, or about four ounces of salt pork; cover with cold water, season with a bay-leaf, a sprig of thyme, two of parsley, two middling-sized onions, with two cloves stuck in them, and a carrot cut in pieces; when the whole is well cooked, throw away thyme, bay-leaf, onions, and cloves; mash well through a colander all the rest except the bacon.

While mashing them through the colander, wet them with some of the water in which they have boiled, else it would be difficult and long.

When mashed, put them in a saucepan with a little broth or water, salt, and two ounces of butter; stir now and then till the butter is melted and thoroughly mixed with the rest, and it is ready for use. The quantity of broth or water is according to how thick or thin they are wanted. The salt pork is good to eat.

Of Lentils.—It is made in the same way as that of beans, except that they do not require to be soaked more than five or six hours in cold water.

Of Peas (dry or split).—Proceed as for lentils in every particular.

Of Chestnuts.—Remove the skin of a quart of chestnuts and drop them in boiling water, with a little salt. As soon as the under skin comes off easily, take them from the fire, drain, drop them in cold water, and then remove the under or white skin; put them in a saucepan with about one quart of broth, set on the fire and boil gently till well done, and mash through a colander.

Then put the chestnuts, and what is left of the broth, in a saucepan, set on the fire, stir, add a pinch of sugar and an ounce of butter; give one boil, and it is made.

Of Green Peas.—Wash a quart of green peas in cold water, and drain; put two quarts of cold water on the fire in a saucepan, with a little salt, and at the first boil throw the peas in, season with three or four sprigs of parsley, one of thyme, two onions, and two cloves, a carrot in slices, salt, and pepper; boil till tender. It may take only two minutes, or it may require half an hour, according to how tender the peas are.

Mash through a colander, and finish like purée of beans, using either broth or water. With broth it is richer and better.

Of Lima Beans.—Proceed for green Limas as for green peas.

Of Sweet Corn.—It is made like that of green peas.

Of Asparagus.—Cut the eatable part of the asparagus in pieces, and proceed as for *purée* of green peas.

Of Potatoes.—Steam a quart of potatoes, and then mash them well; put them in a saucepan with half a pint of milk, two ounces of butter, and salt; set on the fire, stir now and then, take off and use. It takes about fifteen minutes after being set back on the fire.

Another way.—Proceed as above, using broth or water instead of milk.

Of Jerusalem Artichokes.—Prepared as potatoes.

Of Carrots.—Clean well, and cut in slices, a dozen middling-sized carrots; put them in a stewpan with four ounces of butter, and set on the fire; when about half fried, cover with broth or water; season with half a bay-leaf, a small sprig of thyme, one of parsley, a small onion, and a clove stuck in it; when the whole is well cooked, throw away onion, clove, bay-leaf, and thyme, mash the rest through a colander; then put back on the fire, with a little butter; simmer for about two hours, stirring occasionally, and it is made.

In case it should turn too thick, add broth or water.

The longer they are simmered, the better the taste.

Of Turnips.—Proceed as with carrots in every particular.

Of Celery.—It is always made with turnip-rooted celery. Clean the celery well, wash and cut it in pieces, and prepare as *purée of carrots*, adding a teaspoonful of sugar.

Of Cauliflowers.—Separate the branches, and throw them in boiling water and salt; boil two minutes and drain. Put them on the fire with broth or water, enough just to cover them, two or three stalks of parsley, and salt to season.

Boil gently till tender; remove the parsley; mash through a colander; put back on the fire with a little butter and white pepper, simmer about ten minutes, stirring now and then the while, and it is ready for use.

Instead of butter, some cream may be added.

Of Pumpkin.—Made exactly the same as that of cauliflowers, after the pumpkin is peeled and cut in pieces.

Of Squash.—Same as pumpkin.

Of Spinach.—Clean the spinach, and cut off the stem; the leaf only is good; wash and drain it; put cold water and a little salt on the fire, and throw the spinach in at the first boil. When tender, drain and drop immediately in cold water; drain again, and then chop it very fine. After being chopped, it may be mashed through a sieve, to have it finer; put it back on the fire without any water at all, and when it gets rather dry, add a little flour; stir and mix; add again a little gravy or good broth; stir, then salt to taste, and it is ready for use.

If the spinach is young and tender, it takes only two or three minutes boiling before chopping it.

From the time it is put back on the fire, it takes about five or six minutes to finish it.

Of Sorrel.—Proceed as with spinach in every particular.

Of Mushrooms.—Clean well and cut in pieces a quart of fresh mushrooms; soak them in cold water, in which you have put the juice of a lemon; drain, and chop them fine. Put a stewpan on the fire, with a piece of butter the size of a duck's egg; when melted, put your mushrooms in; when half fried, add the juice of a lemon, finish frying, then cover with some roux-sauce; let simmer till it becomes rather thick, strain and use.

Of Onions.—Peel, quarter, and blanch for eight minutes, a dozen onions. Drain and put them in a saucepan with four or six ounces of butter, according to the size of the onions; set on a slow fire, stir now and then till well done; then season with salt, a little flour, stir for two minutes to cook the flour, and mix it thoroughly with the rest; take from the fire; add cream, little by little, stirring the while. It does not require much cream to make the *purée* of a proper thickness. Mash through a sieve or fine colander, add a pinch of sugar, and it is ready for use.

It makes an excellent *purée*, and is good served with nearly every kind of meat.

Made with white onions, and properly mashed through a sieve, it looks like cream, and is almost as white as snow.

FISH.

The Indians bleed the fish as soon as caught, because the flesh is firmer when cooked.

The Dutch and the French bleed the cod, which accounts for the better quality and whiteness of their cod-fish.

To select.—To be good, fish must be fresh. It is fresh when the eyes are clear, the fins stiff, the gills red, hard to open, and without bad odor.

To clean and prepare for boiling.—The sooner fish is cleaned the better. Cut the belly open, take the inside out, wash well and wipe dry immediately with a clean towel, inside and out. Place the eggs or soft roes inside, and tie with twine. It is then ready to be boiled.

If not cooked as soon as cleaned and prepared, keep it on ice.

To clean and prepare for baking, frying, roasting, and to cut in pieces, etc.—Scale the fish well, holding it by the head or tail; cut the belly open and take the inside out; trim off the fins, gills, and tail; wash well inside and out, and wipe dry immediately.

Keep it on ice if not used immediately.

Same Family, or Kind.—We give only one receipt for all the fishes of the same family, or having the same kind of flesh, as they are cooked alike, and require the same spices.

Almost every kind of fish is boiled, broiled, fried, or stewed. Some are better boiled than broiled, others better fried than stewed, etc. With few exceptions, any eatable fish may be cooked in these four ways. Few are roasted.

To know when cooked enough.—It is very difficult, if not entirely impossible, to tell how long it takes to cook fish, as it depends as much on the size, kind, or quality of the fish as on the fire; but as soon as the flesh comes off the bones easily, the fish is cooked; this is very easy to be ascertained with a knife.

To improve.—Clean the fish as for baking, etc., and lay it in a crockery vessel with the following seasonings under and upon it: parsley and onions chopped fine, salt, pepper, thyme, bay-leaves, and vinegar or oil; turn it over occasionally, and leave thus for two or three hours.

To bone.—Slit the fish on one side of the backbone and fins, from head to tail; then run the knife between the bones and the flesh so as to detach the whole side from the rest; do the same for the other side.

For a flounder, or any other flat fish, slit right in the middle of both sides of the fish so as to make four instead of two pieces.

The head, bones, and fins are not used at all, and are left in one piece.

To serve, when boiled.—The fish is placed on a napkin and on a dish or platter, surrounded with parsley, and the sauce served in a saucer.

To skin.—Take hold of the piece of fish by the smaller end, and with the thumb and forefinger of the left hand; run the knife between the flesh and skin, moving the knife to and fro as if you were sawing. Throw away the skin, and the fish is ready for cooking.

If the skin were breaking, as it happens sometimes, take hold of it again, and proceed as before.

To decorate.—Fish may be decorated with jelly, but it is easier and more sightly with craw-fish. The skewers are stuck in the fish as they are in a *fillet of beef*.

The craw-fish when boiled are red like the lobster, and, besides using them with skewers, some may be placed all around the fish; it is delicate eating as well as sightly. Skewers are never used with fish in *vinaigrette*, or when the fish is cut in pieces. The craw-fish has only to be boiled before using it for decorating fish.

Shrimps and *prawns* are used the same as craw-fish.

Oysters are also used, raw or blanched; run the skewer through a large oyster or craw-fish, then through a slice of truffle; again through an oyster, truffle, etc.; through two, three, or more of each, according to the size of the skewer or of the fish.

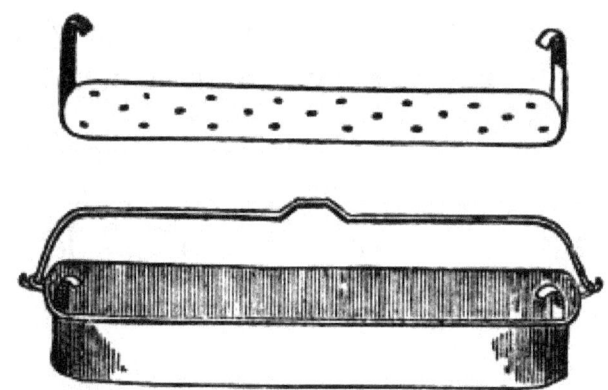

Fish-kettle.—A fish-kettle must have a double bottom. It is more handy to take the fish off without breaking it, and there is no danger of having it spoiled while cooking. Fish-kettles are found in every house-furnishing store.

Baked.—Clean and prepare the fish, as directed for baking; put it in a baking-pan with salt, pepper, and butter spread all over it; just cover the bottom of the pan with water or broth; place a piece of buttered paper over it and bake. Baste two or three times; take off when done, and serve warm with a sauce.

While the fish is baking you prepare the sauce, put it in a boat, and serve warm with the fish.

A baked fish may be served with its gravy only, adding a few drops of lemon-juice or vinegar, or with any kind of sauce, according to taste.

Balls.—Fish-balls are often called *fish-cakes* or *fish-croquettes*. They are generally made with cold fish, but it may be cooked especially to make balls.

Fish, full of bones, like shad, is not fit to make balls; cod is the easiest.

Commence by chopping the flesh very fine, then chop fine also a small piece of onion and fry it with butter (half a middling-sized onion with two ounces of butter are enough for half a pound of fish); when fried stir in it a tablespoonful of flour, and about half a minute after turn the fish in with about a gill of broth or water, salt, pepper, and a pinch of nutmeg; stir till it turns rather thick, which will take two or three minutes; take from the fire, mix two yolks of eggs with it; put back on the fire for about one minute, stirring the while; then add two or three mushrooms or one truffle, or both, chopped fine. Turn the mixture into a dish, spread it, and put it away to cool for two or three hours, or over night.

Before cooking, mix the whole well, the upper part being more dry than that which is under; put it in parts on the paste-board, roll each part to the shape you wish, either round, oval, or flat; the paste-board must be dusted with bread-crumbs or flour to help in handling the mixture, then boil or fry, according to taste.

It may also be baked in cakes.

When fried, they may be dipped in beaten egg, rolled in bread-crumbs, and then fried in hot fat. (*See* FRYING.)

Boiled.—Clean and prepare the fish as directed, and put it in a fish-kettle; cover it with cold water (sea-water is the best); add the following seasonings to a pound of fish: two stalks of parsley, one of tarragon if handy, one tablespoonful of vinegar, and half a middling-sized onion sliced; salt if boiled in fresh water. Set on the fire, and, for a fish weighing two pounds or under, take off at the first boiling—it is done enough. For a fish weighing five pounds, boil five minutes, etc., that is, about one minute for each pound. If it were a thick slice of fish instead of a whole one, weighing two or three pounds, it should be boiled two or three minutes longer, etc., according to thickness.

Broiled.—Slit the fish on the back and clean it; salt and pepper it; have a little melted butter and spread it all over the fish, on both sides, with a brush, and broil it. (*See* BROILING.)

While the fish is broiling, prepare a *maître d'hotel* sauce, spread it on the fish as soon as dished, and serve.

It may also be served with anchovy butter.

Fried.—Any small fish of the size of a smelt, or smaller, is better fried than prepared in any other way.

Clean and prepare the fish as directed, wipe it dry. Dip it in milk, place in a colander for five minutes, then roll in flour, and fry. It may also be fried just rolled in flour.

Another way.—When wiped dry, dip in beaten egg, roll in bread-crumbs, and fry.

Another.—When wiped dry, dip the fish in butter, and fry. Then the fish is dropped in hot fat (*see* FRYING), turned into a colander, salted, and served hot, with fried parsley around or in the middle, according to how the fish is arranged in the dish.

Fry the following as above: *carp, tench, frost, bass, perch, black and blue fish, gold, loach, mullet, porgy, weak, flounder, pike, pickerel, smelt, sun, herring,* and *white-fish of the lakes.*

A la Orly.—If it is small fish, like the smelt, it is prepared whole; if the fish is larger, it must be boned and skinned, and cut in pieces about two inches long. Roll the fish, or pieces of fish, slightly in flour; dip it in beaten egg, and roll it again in bread-crumbs; then fry it in hot fat as above.

When fried, serve it with a tomato-sauce.

The fish may be served on a napkin in a dish, and the sauce in a boat or saucer.

Roasted.—The following fishes only are roasted: *eel, salmon, shad, pike, turbot.*

Clean and prepare as directed, and then tie with twine. Spread salt, pepper, and melted butter (with a brush) all over the fish, and then envelop it in buttered paper; set on the spit and roast. Baste with a little melted butter, and remove the paper about five minutes before it is done.

When on the dish the twine is cut off and removed, and it is served as hot as possible with the following sauces, to which tarragon is added in making them, if handy: *caper, Hollandaise, Mayonnaise, piquante, poivrade,* and *rémolade.* A roast fish is served after roast meat.

Another way.—Clean, and cut in slices half an inch thick, or leave entire, as it suits you; skin it well; lay it in a crockery vessel, spread over it some chopped parsley, grated nutmeg, salt, pepper, and two gills of white wine (this is for about three pounds), leave thus two hours; then take the fish only, envelop it in buttered paper, fix it on the spit before a good fire, baste with the wine and seasonings from the crockery dish, and when nearly done take the paper off; finish the cooking, basting the while, and serve with the drippings, to which you may add a little vinegar, sweet-oil, and mustard.

If there is any left, you can serve it cold the next day with an oil-sauce.

Sauté.—Scale, clean, and prepare the fish as directed. For one pound of fish put about one ounce of butter in a frying-pan on the fire, and when melted put the fish in; fry it on both sides, and serve it with a *maître d'hotel*.

Stewed.—Clean and prepare as directed three pounds of fish, cut it in pieces about two inches long. Put in a fish-kettle four ounces of butter, kneaded with a teaspoonful of flour, and the same of chopped parsley, add two or three mushrooms cut in pieces, salt and pepper, then the fish and a glass of claret wine, or a wine-glass of vinegar; cover with water, set on a good fire, boil gently till cooked; dish the pieces of fish, strain the sauce on them, spread the pieces of mushrooms over, and serve.

Stuffed.—When cleansed, cut out the backbone from the head to within two inches of the tail, and fill its place with the following mixture: soak stale bread in cold water and then squeeze the water out; put one ounce of butter into a saucepan and set it on the fire; as soon as melted, fry in it one middle-sized onion, chopped fine; then add the bread; stir for two minutes, add also salt, pepper, a pinch of nutmeg, two or three tablespoonfuls of broth; stir again two or three minutes; take the pan from the fire, add a yolk of egg, put back on the fire for half a minute, stirring the while, take off again, add a teaspoonful of chopped parsley, and use. When full, tie the fish with twine; place it in a baking-pan, salt and pepper it; spread a little butter on it also; cover the bottom of the pan with cold water, bake and serve with its gravy.

If there is not gravy enough, or if it has dried away, add a little broth a few minutes before taking from the oven.

Fish au Gratin.—Bone and skin the fish as directed. For a fish weighing about two pounds, spread one ounce of butter on a tin plate or baking-pan, spread over it half an onion, chopped; place the pieces of fish on them; add salt, pepper, a tablespoonful of vinegar or a wine-glass of white wine, and half an ounce of butter; spread over and bake.

While it is baking, put in a small saucepan one ounce of butter, and set it on the fire; when melted, add half a tablespoonful of flour, stir, and, when it is turning yellow, add also about one gill of broth, two tablespoonfuls of meat-gravy, the juice of the fish when baked (if the fish be not done when the time comes to put the juice in the pan, keep the pan in a warm place, and wait), salt, and pepper; boil gently about five minutes, stirring occasionally. Place the fish in a tin or silver dish, spread three or four mushrooms sliced over it; turn the sauce gently over the whole, dust with bread-crumbs; put half an ounce of butter, in four or five pieces, on the whole; bake ten or twelve minutes, and serve in the dish in which it is.

In Matelote.—Every kind of fish is good in *matelote*, but the following are the best: *bass*, *black-fish*, *blue-fish*, *carp*, *eel*, *perch*, *pickerel*, *pike*, *porgy*, *tench*, *trout*, and *craw-fish*.

A *matelote* may be made of eels alone, but it is better with eels and one, two, or three other kinds of fish.

Eels tasting of mud are not good. There is a sure way of taking away the muddy taste, but it is a rather expensive one. Boil them a few minutes in claret wine and a little salt, before using them.

Clean, and prepare as directed, one pound of eels, one pound of pike, and one pound of trout, or one pound of any of the fishes named above—in all, three pounds. Cut the fish in pieces about two inches long, fry it slightly with a little butter, and put it away for awhile.

Put four ounces of butter in a saucepan and set it on the fire; when melted, add two tablespoonfuls of flour, stir, and, when the flour is turning rather brown, add also about a quart of broth, a pint of claret, a bunch of seasonings, composed of half a dozen stalks of parsley, two of thyme, two bay-leaves, and two cloves, also salt, pepper, two cloves of garlic, and six button onions; boil gently for about half an hour. Then put the fish in with from six to twelve mushrooms, broth enough to cover the whole, if the broth and wine already in do not cover it; boil gently for about half an hour, or till the fish is cooked, tossing the saucepan now and then; dish the fish; place the mushrooms and onions all over; sprinkle the sauce over it through a strainer, and serve warm. *Croutons* may be served around.

Another, or Marinière.—Prepare and cut the fish as for the above, but instead of frying it put it in a saucepan, into which you have put previously about half a dozen sprigs of parsley, two of thyme, two bay-leaves, two cloves of garlic, twelve small onions, two cloves, salt, and pepper; when the fish is placed over the above seasonings, cover entirely with claret wine. Set the saucepan on a sharp fire, and, as soon as it boils, throw into it a glass of French brandy, set it on fire, and let it burn. It will not burn very long, but enough to give a good taste to it. As soon as it stops burning, knead four ounces of butter with a tablespoonful of flour, and put it in the pan; toss the pan gently now and then till done. It takes about forty minutes with a good fire.

When done, dish the fish carefully, place the mushrooms all over it, the onions all around, strain the sauce over the whole, and serve warm.

Croutons may also be served with the rest; put around the fish one *crouton*, then an onion, and so on, all around.

Another.—Proceed as for the above, in every particular, except that you cover the fish and seasonings with broth and white wine, half of each, instead of claret. Serve in the same way.

A *matelote* may be made three or four days in advance, and then warmed in boiling water (*bain-marie*) just before serving it.

Many prefer a *matelote* made four days before eating it, and prepared in the following way: When made, put it away to cool as quickly as possible; twenty-four hours after that, warm it in boiling water; cool, and warm again in the same way once a day. If the sauce becomes thick, add a little broth. Serve warm.

Vinaigrette.—Boil a fish as directed, take it from the kettle and let cool; then dish it. Chop fine the yolks of two hard-boiled eggs; do the same with the two whites; chop also a handful of parsley. Put a string of the yolks on both sides of the fish, then along that a string of the whites, and along these a string of the parsley; along the parsley, and about half an inch apart, a string of capers. Cut a lemon in sixteen slices, and in the following way: first split the lemon in two lengthwise, then split again each half in two and lengthwise also; by splitting four times, you have sixteen pieces, resembling somewhat the carpels of oranges. After the first splitting, hold the piece of lemon with the nail of the left thumb, the rind downward, and always split lengthwise and in the middle. Place eight pieces on each side of the dish and along the capers, and serve cold, with stalks of parsley on top of the fish, and also two or three in its mouth.

Serve with it a vinaigrette, in a saucer or boat.

The following fishes, *bass, black and blue fish, carp, cat, dory, drum, gar, gurnard, herring, king, lump, mackerel, parr, perch, pickerel, pike, pilot, porgy, roach, rock, scup, sucker, sword, tautog, tench, trout, troutlet, weak,* and *weaver,* after being baked or boiled as directed, may be served with the following sauces: *anchovy, caper, génevoise, génoise, au gratin, Hollandaise, Italienne, matelote, tomato, Tartar,* and *vinaigrette*.

It would be perfectly useless to have a receipt for each fish, since the preparation is the same.

The same fishes are also prepared *au court bouillon*. Clean and prepare about three pounds of fish, as directed for baking, etc. It may be one fish or several, according to size. Place the fish in a fish-kettle, just cover it with cold water and a gill of vinegar, or with half water and half white wine; season with three or four sprigs of parsley, one of thyme, a bay-leaf, one clove, one onion, half a carrot (in slices), two cloves of garlic, salt, pepper, and a little tarragon, if handy. Set on the fire, and boil gently till done. Dish the fish, and serve it warm with a caper or anchovy sauce in a boat, or with currant jelly.

The same—à la Bretonne.—Slit the fish on the back, as for broiling, and clean it. When wiped dry, lay it in a bake-pan in which there is a little melted butter, the inside of the fish under; place thus on a good fire, turn over when done on one side, and, when cooked, spread some *maître d'hôtel* on it, and serve warm.

The same—aux fines herbes.—Clean and prepare as for baking, etc., and also improve it as directed. Envelop the fish in buttered paper, and also the seasonings in which it has been improved, except the thyme and bay-leaves, broil it, and serve with *piquante* sauce.

Cod-fish, *cusk*, *haddock*, *hake*, *halibut*, *pollack*, and *torsk*, after being baked or boiled as directed, are served with the following sauces:

Anchovy, Béchamel, caper, cream, egg, Hollandaise, maître d'hôtel, tomato, vinaigrette.

EEL, CONGER, AND LAMPREY.

To clean.—When skinned, clean, head, and tail them. Then throw them in boiling water, in which you have put a little salt and a teaspoonful of vinegar; leave them in it about five minutes, take out, and drain.

Broiled.—Clean and cut two pounds of eel, or of either of the others, in pieces about three inches long. Put in a stewpan a piece of butter the size of an egg, and set it on the fire; when hot, lay the eels in, fry about three minutes, turning them over the while; then turn the whole into a crockery vessel, add a teaspoonful of chopped parsley and onions, a pinch of grated nutmeg, a tablespoonful of sweet-oil, salt, and pepper; set on the fire and simmer two hours; take off, roll the pieces in fine bread-crumbs, place them on a gridiron, and on a good fire, and serve when done with *piquante* sauce.

From the nature of their flesh, eels require to be prepared thus; and, when properly done, make really a very good dish.

Roasted.—Prepare the eels as for broiling, and, instead of placing on the gridiron, envelop them in oiled paper and roast before a sharp fire. Serve with *piquante, ravigote,* or Tartar sauce.

Fried.—Prepare as for broiling as far as rolling in bread-crumbs, then dip in beaten-egg, roll in bread-crumbs again, and fry. (*See* Frying.) Serve with tomato-sauce, or just as it is.

In Maître d'hôtel.—Clean as directed, but boil twenty minutes instead of five. Serve with a *maître d'hôtel* sauce and steamed potatoes, or with muscle, oyster, shrimp, or Tartar sauce.

In Matelote.—(*See* Fish in Matelote.)

Stuffed.—Clean as directed; stuff it with currant jelly, bake or roast, and serve with currant jelly.

Flounder (wrongly called *sole*; the flounder is as good as the sole—the soles that may be found here are imported from Europe or from Newfoundland), *dab-fish*, and *plaice*, after being baked or boiled, may be served with the following sauces:

Allemande, anchovy, anchovy-butter, Mayonnaise, tomato, and *au gratin.*

Baked.—Clean three pounds of the above fish. Put in a crockery dish four ounces of butter, set it on a good fire, and when melted sprinkle in it a teaspoonful of flour, stirring the while; also, a pinch of grated nutmeg, salt, pepper, a saltspoonful of chopped parsley, two or three mushrooms, also chopped, then the fish; pour on it a glass of white wine, and a liquor-glass of French brandy; cover the dish, take it from the fire, and put it in a moderately heated oven, and serve when done just as it is, and in the crockery dish.

A la Normande.—Bone and skin the fish as directed. For a fish weighing four pounds, spread two ounces of butter on the bottom of a baking-pan; spread one onion, chopped fine, over the butter, and as much carrot, cut in small dice. Place the fish over the whole, the pieces as they are, or cut according to the size of the pan, salt and pepper, and bake. Take from the oven when done and dish the fish, leaving the juice in the pan; cut the stems of about a dozen mushrooms; place the heads on the middle of the fish, and the stems around it.

Mix cold a tablespoonful of flour and the same of butter in a saucepan, turn into it a pint of broth, set on the fire and stir continually; when thoroughly mixed, turn into it also, and through a strainer, the juice from the pan in which the fish has baked; stir again two or three minutes; turn gently over the fish, put in the oven for about ten minutes, and serve hot. *Croutons* may be placed around the dish as a decoration.

Another Normande.—Bone and skin the fish as directed; butter well the dish on which the fish is to be served, spread some chopped onion all over, then place the fish over it; sprinkle salt, pepper, and white wine or vinegar (a tablespoonful to a pound of fish), all over the fish, and bake it. It takes about fifteen minutes for a fish weighing two or three pounds. Wine is better than vinegar.

While the fish is baking, set a saucepan on the fire with an ounce of butter in it, and when melted, add half a tablespoonful of flour; stir, and when turning yellow, add also half a pint of broth or water, salt, then the juice from the fish when baked, stir, give one boil, and turn over the fish.

Blanch a dozen or so of oysters, place them all over the fish also.

Have ready two or three potatoes, cut with a round vegetable spoon; boil till done; place them around the fish as a border for it; dust then the whole with bread-crumbs, put in a warm oven for about fifteen minutes, take off, place half a dozen *croutons* all around the dish also, and serve.

The *croutons* are generally cut of a heart-shape. It will be easily done if the directions are followed properly and carefully.

Commence by cutting the bread, then cut the potatoes, and set them on the fire with cold water and salt; while they are cooking, prepare the fish and set it in the oven; while this is baking, make the sauce, fry the *croutons*, and blanch the oysters. If the fish is baked before the rest are ready, take it off and keep warm till wanted. It makes a sightly and excellent dish.

The same fried.—Small flounders are fried like other small fish, and served either with or without a tomato-sauce or *à la Orly*.

The same, boned and fried.—Bone and skin small flounders as directed; mix together a tablespoonful of oil, a teaspoonful of chopped parsley, the juice of half a lemon, and salt; dip the pieces of fish in the mixture, dust them slightly with flour, and fry. Serve hot.

Pike, Pickerel, and Trout or Troutlet.—Those three fish, besides being prepared as directed for bass, etc., and in all its different ways, they are boiled as directed and served warm, with a *génoise* sauce.

A more delicious dish of fish can hardly be prepared.

Ray, Skate, and Angel or Monk fish.—Ray, though excellent, is very little known; there is only one place at which it can be bought—Washington Market, New York.

It is unquestionably an excellent dish, prepared *au beurre noir*. When clean, boil the fish as directed, and dish it, sprinkling salt and pepper on it.

While it is boiling, put about two ounces of butter to a pound of fish in a frying-pan, set it on a sharp fire, stir now and then, and when brown, throw into it about six sprigs of parsley, which you take off immediately with a skimmer. As soon as the parsley is taken off, pour the butter over the fish, quickly put two tablespoonfuls of vinegar in the frying-pan and over the fire, give one boil, and pour also over the fish. Frying the parsley and boiling the vinegar cannot be done too fast, as the fish must be served very warm. The warmer it is served, the better it is.

Salmon, sturgeon, and *white-fish,* after being baked or boiled, may be served with a caper, and also with a *Mayonnaise* sauce. They may also be served in *court bouillon,* like bass. They are broiled whole, or in slices, and served with a *maître d'hôtel* or a caper sauce.

The same in Fricandeau.—Cut the fish in slices about half an inch thick, and place them in a saucepan with slices of fat salt pork, carrots and onions under them; set on a good fire; ten minutes after, add a little broth, just enough to cover the bottom of the pan; after about five minutes, turn the slices over; finish the cooking and serve with the gravy strained over the fish, or with a tomato-sauce.

The same in Papillotes.—Fry slices of salmon with a little butter, and until of a golden color; take them from the fire. While they are frying, mix well together parsley chopped fine, salt, pepper, melted butter, grated nutmeg, and a little lemon-juice; spread some of the mixture on both sides of the slices of fish, envelop them in buttered or oiled paper; broil, and serve them hot.

Some mushrooms or truffles, or both, and chopped, may be added to the mixture.

The same à la Génevoise.—Put in a saucepan a thick slice of salmon—from five to six pounds; just cover it with broth and claret wine—half of each; season with a bunch of seasonings composed of six or eight sprigs of parsley, two of thyme, two bay-leaves, two cloves, and two cloves of garlic, salt, a few slices of carrot, and a small green onion, or a shallot, if handy. Boil gently till nearly done, when add about a dozen mushrooms, and keep boiling till done; dish the fish, and put it in a warm but not hot place; mix cold, in a saucepan, four ounces of butter with about two ounces of flour; turn over it, through a strainer, the liquor in which the fish has been cooked, and set on a sharp fire; after about three minutes, during which you have stirred with a wooden spoon, add the mushrooms; stir again for about two minutes, turn over the fish, and serve warm.

The same in Salad.—Boil, as directed for fish, some thin slices of salmon, drain, and serve cold, on a napkin and on a dish.

Serve with it, and in a boat, the following: half a teaspoonful of salt, a pinch of pepper, two tablespoonfuls of vinegar, four of sweet oil, a pickled cucumber chopped fine, two hard-boiled eggs, chopped fine also, two or three anchovies, and a tablespoonful of capers; the anchovies may be chopped fine or pounded. Beat the whole well and serve.

The same in Scallops.—Cut it in round slices, about one-eighth of an inch in thickness; fry them with butter, and serve.

The pieces should be tastefully arranged on a dish, imitating a flight of stairs.

Broiled.—Cut it in rather thin slices, butter both sides with a brush; broil, and serve with a *maître d'hôtel*.

Shad and *sheep's-head*, after being baked or boiled, are served with an anchovy, caper, or tomato sauce. They are also served cold, *à la vinaigrette*.

Broiled.—When cleaned and prepared, salt, pepper, and butter it; broil and serve it with a *maître d'hôtel*.

It may be *stuffed* as directed for fish.

In Provençale.—Clean, prepare, and cut the fish in pieces about two inches long; put about three pounds of it in a saucepan, with a pint of claret; six stalks of parsley, a small onion, a clove of garlic, and six mushrooms, all chopped fine; boil till done, when add four ounces of butter, and two of flour, well kneaded together; boil three minutes longer, and serve warm.

Another way, or à la Chambord.—Stuff the fish with sausage-meat, envelop it in a towel, boil, and serve it with a tomato-sauce.

The same with Sorrel.—Broil the fish, and serve it on a purée of sorrel or of spinach.

It may also be prepared *au court bouillon, à la Bretonne,* and *aux fines herbes,* like bass, etc.

Sheep's-head may also be prepared like turbot.

Au Gratin.—The shad, after being cleaned, but not split on the back (as is too often the case, to the shame of the fishmongers who begin by spoiling the fish under the pretence of cleaning it), is placed in a bake-pan, having butter, chopped parsley, mushroom, salt, and pepper, both under and above the fish. For a fish weighing three pounds, add one gill of broth and half as much of white wine; dust the fish with bread-crumbs, and set in a pretty quick oven.

Fifteen minutes afterward, examine it. When done, the fish is dished, a little broth is put in the pan, which is placed on a sharp fire; stir with a spoon or fork so as to detach the bread, etc., that may stick to the pan, then pour this over the fish, and serve warm.

The gravy must be reduced to two or three tablespoonfuls only, for a fish weighing about two pounds.

The fish must be dished carefully in order not to break it.

Sterlet.—This is a fish of the sturgeon family, very plentiful in the Caspian Sea and in many Russian rivers, principally in the Neva and in Lake Ladoga.

Tunny and *bonito*, after being boiled, are served cold in *vinaigrette*.

Turbot and Whiff.—Turbot is among fishes what pheasant is among birds. Rub it with lemon before cooking it.

After being boiled or baked, as directed, it is served with the following sauces: *Béchamel, cream, caper, Hollandaise, Mayonnaise, tomato,* and in *vinaigrette.*

It is also served *au court-bouillon* and *aux fines herbes* like bass.

Au Gratin.—It is prepared and served like shad au gratin.

It is also broiled and served with a *maître d'hôtel.*

Bordelaise.—Bone and skin the fish as directed; dip each piece in melted butter, then in beaten egg, roll in bread-crumbs and broil. While it is broiling on a rather slow fire, turn it over several times and keep basting with melted butter; the more butter it absorbs the better the fish.

When broiled, serve the slices on a dish and place some boiled craw-fish all around and in the middle. A dish of steamed potatoes is served with it.

The following sauce is also served at the same time: Chop fine and fry till half done, with a little butter, two small green onions or four shallots. Put half a pint of good meat-gravy in a small saucepan; set on the fire, and as soon as it commences to boil, pour into it, little by little, stirring the while with a wooden spoon, about a gill of Bordeaux wine, then the onions or shallots, and also a piece of beef marrow chopped fine; give one boil, and serve in a saucer.

In Salad.—Proceed as for salmon in salad.

When *boiled,* serve the turbot with anchovy-butter, lobster-butter, lobster-sauce, or muscle-sauce.

Cold.—Any cold piece of turbot is served with a *Mayonnaise* sauce, or in *vinaigrette.*

Cold Fish.—If the fish is with sauce, that is, if the sauce is in the same dish with the fish, warm it in the *bain-marie,* and serve warm. Any other piece of cold fish, baked, boiled, broiled, or roasted, is served with a *Mayonnaise* sauce, or with a *vinaigrette.*

Any kind of cold fish may be prepared in salad. Slice the fish or cut it in pieces and put it in the salad-dish with hard-boiled egg sliced, onion and parsley chopped fine, salt, pepper, vinegar, and oil. Mix the whole gently and well, and serve.

Anchovy.—It is imported preserved. It is used as a *hors-d'oeuvre*, to decorate or season.

The essence of anchovy is used for sauce.

The smallest are considered the best.

To serve as a *hors d'oeuvre*, wash, wipe dry, and remove the backbone, serve with tarragon or parsley, chopped fine, vinegar, and oil.

They may also be served with hard-boiled eggs, chopped or quartered.

Sprats.—There are none in or near American waters; they are imported under their French name, sardines. Fresh sprats are very good boiled without any grease, and without being cleaned and prepared like other fish; but when on the plate, skin them, which is easily done, as then the flesh is so easily detached from the bones that the inside need not be touched at all; they are eaten with salt and pepper only.

Sardines are served as a *hors-d'oeuvre*, with oil and lemon-juice, and properly scaled. They are arranged on the dish according to fancy, together with lemon in slices.

Salt Cod—to prepare.—Soak it in cold water for two days, changing the water two or three times; then scale it well and clean. Lay it in a fish-kettle, cover with cold water, set on a rather slow fire, skim off the scum, let it boil about one minute, take the kettle from the fire, cover it well, and leave thus ten minutes; then take off the cod, and drain it.

In Béchamel.—Prepare it as above, and serve with a béchamel sauce, and as warm as possible.

With a Cream-Sauce.—Prepare as above, and serve either warm or cold with a cream-sauce.

In Brown Butter.—When prepared as above, place it on a dish, and keep it in a warm place. Put four ounces of butter in a frying-pan, and on a good fire; when turning brown, add three sprigs of parsley, fry about two minutes, pour the whole on the fish, and serve. You may also pour on it a hot caper-sauce, and serve.

With Croutons.—Prepare and cook as directed, three pounds of cod; take the bones out, break in small pieces, and mash with the hand as much as possible; put it then in a stewpan, beat three yolks of eggs with two tablespoonfuls of cream, and mix with the cod; set on a slow fire, and immediately pour in, little by little, stirring the while, about one gill of sweet oil; simmer ten or twelve minutes, and serve with *croutons* around.

In Maître d'Hôtel.—Lay three pounds of cod on a dish, after being cooked as directed; keep it warm, spread a *maître d'hôtel* sauce on it, and serve.

With Potatoes.—Prepare about three pounds of cod as directed above. Lay the fish on a dish; have a *piquante* sauce ready, turn it over it, and serve with steamed potatoes all around the dish. The potatoes may also be served separately.

In Vinaigrette.—Prepare as directed, and when cold, serve with a vinaigrette.

With Cheese.—Prepare the cod as directed, then dip it in lukewarm butter, roll it in grated cheese, lay it in a baking-pan, dust slightly with bread-crumbs; bake, and serve warm. Two or three minutes in a quick oven will be sufficient.

Au Gratin.—When soaked only and wiped dry, but not boiled, prepare it as directed for fish au gratin.

With Caper-Sauce.—Prepare it as directed, and serve warm with caper-sauce.

Salt Salmon.—Soak it in cold water for some time, the length of time to be according to the saltness of the fish; scale and clean it well, lay it in a fish-kettle, cover it with cold water, and set it on a moderate fire. Boil gently about two minutes, skim off the scum, take from the kettle and drain it. Put butter in a frying-pan and set it on the fire; when it turns rather brown, put a few sprigs of parsley in it, and immediately pour it over the fish in the dish; add a few drops of lemon-juice all over, and serve warm.

It may also be served with a caper or *maître d'hôtel* sauce; or, when cold, serve *à la vinaigrette*.

Salt salmon is also served like salt cod-fish.

It may also be served on a *purée* of celery or of onion.

Smoked Salmon.—Cut it in thin slices; have very hot butter or oil in a frying-pan, and lay the slices in only long enough to warm them; then take out, drain them, and serve with a few drops of lemon-juice or vinegar sprinkled on them.

Tunny.—This is not a good fish fresh; it is generally preserved, and served as a *hors-d'oeuvre*. It comes from Holland, Italy, and the south of France.

Fresh, it is prepared like sturgeon. That prepared in Holland is the best. The Dutch cure fish better than any other nation.

When you serve tunny, take it out of the bottle or jar and serve it on a small plate, or on a dessert-plate. A very small piece is served, generally like every other *hors-d'oeuvre*.

Salt Herring.—Soak in cold or tepid water; if soaked in tepid water, it does not require as long; the time must be according to the quality or saltness of the fish. Wipe dry, broil, and serve like salt mackerel.

Another way.—Salt herring may also be soaked in half water and half milk, or in milk only; drain and wipe dry. Bone and skin, cut off the head, tail, and fins, and serve with oil, vinegar, and pickled cucumbers.

They are also served with slices of sour apples, or slices of onions, after being soaked and wiped dry.

They may also be broiled slightly and served with oil only, after being soaked, or served with sour grape-juice.

Salt Pike.—It is prepared and served the same as salt herring; so is pickled trout.

Red Herring.—Wipe or skin them, they are not as good when washed; cut off the head and tail, split the back open, lay them on a warm and well-greased gridiron, set on a slow fire; spread some butter or oil on them, turn over, do the same on the other side; broil very little, and serve with a *vinaigrette* and mustard to taste.

Another way.—Clean and split them as above, soak them in lukewarm water for two hours; take out, drain, and wipe dry. Mix two or three yolks of eggs with a teaspoonful of chopped parsley, salt, pepper, and a little melted butter; put some of the mixture around every herring, then roll them in fine bread-crumbs, place them on a gridiron on a slow fire: and when lightly broiled, serve as the preceding one.

Red herring may also be broiled with bread-crumbs like salt herring.

It is also served as a *hors-d'oeuvre*, cut in slices.

Salt Mackerel broiled.—If the fish be too salt, soak it for a while in lukewarm water, take off and wipe dry. Have a little melted fat or lard, dip a brush in it and grease slightly both sides of the fish; place on or inside of the gridiron, the bars of which must also be greased; set on, or before, or under a pretty sharp fire; broil both sides; dish the fish, the skin under; spread butter on it; also parsley chopped fine, and serve.

Lemon-juice may be added if liked, or a few drops of vinegar.

When broiled and dished, spread a *maître d'hôtel* on it, and serve.

Another way.—When soaked and wiped dry, dip in melted butter, again in beaten eggs, and roll in bread-crumbs. Broil and serve with parsley and lemon-juice, or with a *maître d'hôtel*.

FROGS.

The hind-legs of frogs only are used as food; formerly they were eaten by the French only, but now, frog-eating has become general, and the Americans are not behind any others in relishing that kind of food.

Fried.—Skin well, and throw into boiling water with a little salt, for five minutes, the hind-legs only; take out and throw them in cold water to cool, and drain. Have hot fat in a pan on the fire (*see* Directions for Frying); lay the frogs in, and serve when done with fried parsley around.

Stewed.—Skin, boil five minutes, throw in cold water, and drain as above. Put in a stewpan two ounces of butter (for two dozen frogs); set it on the fire, and when melted, lay the legs in, fry two minutes, tossing now and then; then sprinkle on them a teaspoonful of flour, stir with a wooden spoon, add two sprigs of parsley, one of thyme, a bay-leaf, two cloves, one of garlic, salt, white pepper, and half a pint of white wine; boil gently till done, dish the legs, reduce the sauce on the fire, strain it, mix in it two yolks of eggs, pour on the legs, and serve them.

LOBSTER.

Never buy a dead lobster.

Large lobsters are not as good as small ones. From about one to two pounds and a half in weight are the best. The heavier the better.

Lobsters are better at some seasons of the year than at others. They are inferior when full of eggs.

It is from mere prejudice that the liver (also called *tomalley*) is eschewed. This prejudice may come from its turning green on boiling the lobster.

Use every thing but the stomach and the black of bluish vein running along its back and tail.

Boil your lobsters yourself; because, if you buy them already boiled, you do not know if they were alive when put in the kettle.

A lobster boiled after being dead is watery, soft, and not full; besides being very unhealthy, if not dangerous.

A lobster suffers less by being put in cold than in boiling water, and the flesh is firmer when done. In putting it in boiling water it is killed by the heat; in cold water it is dead as soon as the water gets warm.

To boil..—Lay it in a fish-kettle; just cover it with cold water, cover the kettle, and set it on a sharp fire.

It takes from fifteen to twenty-five minutes' boiling, according to the size of the lobster.

When boiled, take it from the kettle, break it in two, that is, separate the body from the tail, and place it in a colander to let the water drain.

In the shell.—When the lobster is boiled, divide it in two, taking care not to break the body and large claws. The tail is then split in two, lengthwise, the flesh taken off, cut in small dice, and mixed with the inside of the lobster.

The vein found immediately under the shell, all along the flesh of the lobster, is removed as soon as it is split. The stomach, found near the head, is removed also and thrown away; all the rest is good, including the liver.

When the flesh and inside are properly mixed, season with salt, pepper, vinegar, oil, mustard, and chopped parsley.

Place the body of the lobster on the middle of a dish, the head up, the two large claws stretched out, and the two feelers stretched out also and fastened between the claws. A sprig of parsley is put in each claw, at the end of it, in the small claws as well as in the two large ones. Then the two empty halves of the tail-piece are put around the body of the lobster, the prepared flesh placed around them; hard-boiled eggs cut in eight pieces each are placed around the dish, tastefully arranged; some slices of red, pickled beets and cut with paste-cutters, are placed between each piece of egg, and serve.

It makes a simple, good, and very sightly dish.

Half a dozen boiled craw-fish may be placed around the dish also; it will add to the decoration.

Two middling-sized lobsters prepared thus will fill a very large dish. They should be placed back to back, with only a few craw-fish between, and the rest arranged as the above.

In Salad.—Boil the lobster as directed; break and drain it as directed also. Slice the flesh of the tail, place it tastefully on a dish; also the flesh from the two large claws, which may be sliced or served whole. Lettuce, or hard-boiled eggs, or both, may be arranged on the dish also, and served with the following sauce:

Put in a boat or saucer all the inside save the stomach, with salt, pepper, vinegar, oil, mustard, and chopped parsley, to taste; beat and mix the whole well together, and serve. In case there are eggs, these are also to be mixed with the rest.

Another.—Boil and drain as directed; cut all the flesh in dice, and put it in a bowl with the inside, some lettuce cut rather fine, salt, pepper, vinegar, mustard, and very little oil; mix well, and then put the mixture on a dish, placing it like a mound on the middle of the dish; spread a *Mayonnaise* sauce over it; decorate with the centre leaves of the lettuce, some hard-boiled eggs cut in slices or in fancy shapes, capers, boiled or pickled red beets, cut also in fancy shapes, slices of lemon, and serve.

Anchovies, olives, pickled cucumbers, or any other pickled fruit or vegetable may also be added.

A rose, or two or three pinks, may be placed right on the top, as a decoration. Just before commencing to serve, the rose may be put on a dessert plate and offered to a lady.

In Coquilles, or Scalloped.—It is boiled and then finished like oysters scalloped.

It may be served thus on scallop-shells, on silver shells, or on its own shell; that is, on the shell of the tail, split in two lengthwise, and trimmed according to fancy.

Croquettes.—Lobster croquettes are made exactly like *fish-balls*, and then fried according to directions for frying.

They are served warm. It is an excellent dish for *breakfast*.

Fried.—To be fried, the lobster must be bled; separate the body from the tail, then cut the tail in pieces, making as many pieces as there are joints. Put these pieces in a frying-pan with two or three ounces of butter, and one onion, chopped fine; set on a sharp fire, stir now and then tin the whole is fried, then add a bunch of seasoning composed of three sprigs of parsley, one of thyme, a bay-leaf, and a clove; salt, pepper, and three gills of Madeira wine; boil gently till reduced about half; dish the pieces of lobster according to fancy; add two or three tablespoonfuls of gravy to the sauce, stir it, give one boil, and turn it over the lobster through a strainer; serve warm.

Another way.—Proceed as above in every particular, except that you use Sauterne or Catawba wine instead of Madeira, and, besides the seasonings, add half a dozen mushrooms, or two truffles, or both.

Dish the mushrooms and truffles with the lobster, then finish and serve as the above.

Craw-fish.—These are found in most of the lakes, brooks, and rivers.

In some places they are called *river-crabs*, or freshwater crabs.

They resemble the lobster, and are often taken for young lobsters.

Besides being a beautiful ornament and much used to decorate dishes, they are excellent to eat and very light.

They are dressed and served like lobsters and crabs.

Fishermen are sure to find a ready market for them, though they are, as yet, very little known.

Crabs.—Crabs are boiled like lobsters, and may be served like lobster, *in salad*. They are often eaten, only boiled, without any seasonings.

Like lobsters also, to be good, crabs must be put in the water alive.

When well washed and clean, they may be prepared in the following way: Put them in a saucepan with slices of onions, same of carrots, parsley, chives if handy, thyme, bay-leaves, cloves, salt, and pepper-corns; half cover them with white wine, add butter, set on a good fire, and boil till done. Serve with parsley only.

The sauce may be used a second time by adding a little wine.

The *soft-shell crab* is blanched five minutes, and *fried* like fish.

It may also be *sauté* with a little butter, and served with a *maître d'hôtel*.

Broil it also, and serve it with a *maître d'hôtel*.

Muscles.—These are unwholesome between April and September. They must be heavy, fresh, and of a middling size. The very large ones are really inferior.

Soak them in water and wash well several times, then drain.

In Poulette.—Put them in a saucepan with a little parsley chopped fine, and set them on a pretty good fire; as soon as they are opened, remove the shell to which they are not attached, and keep them in a warm place.

For two quarts of muscles, put two ounces of butter in the saucepan in which they have been cooked and in which you have left their liquor; set on the fire, stir, and as soon as the butter is melted, add and stir into it a tablespoonful of flour; when turning a little yellow, add also half a dozen pepper-corns, then the muscles; boil gently about ten minutes, stirring occasionally; take from the fire, mix one or two yolks of eggs with it, a little lemon-juice, parsley chopped fine, and serve warm.

Another way.—When clean, put them in a saucepan with a few slices of carrot, same of onion, two or three stalks of parsley, one of thyme, a bay-leaf, two cloves, six pepper-corns, and salt. Set on the fire, and take the muscles from the pan as soon as they open, then remove one shell; put them back in the pan, with as much white wine as there is liquor from the muscles; boil gently about ten minutes, add the yolk of an egg, a little lemon-juice, and dish the muscles; drain the sauce over them, add a little chopped parsley, and serve warm.

Fried.—Fry, and serve the muscles like fried oysters. They may also be served like scalloped oysters.

Prawns and Shrimps.—Wash, boil in water and salt, and serve. They may be used, like craw-fish, to decorate fish after being boiled.

Another way.—Wash well, and put two quarts of them in a saucepan with four onions in slices, two sprigs of parsley, one of thyme, a bay-leaf, two cloves, salt, pepper, half a pint of white wine, and two ounces of butter, just cover with water and set on a good fire; when properly cooked, drain, and serve warm with green parsley all around. The liquor may be used a second time.

OYSTERS.

The American oyster is unquestionably the best that can be found. It varies in taste according to how it is treated, either after being dredged or while embedded; and also according to the nature of the soil and water in which they have lived. It is very wrong to wash oysters. We mean by washing oysters, the abominable habit of throwing oysters in cold water, as soon as opened, and then sold by the measure. It is more than a pity to thus spoil such an excellent and delicate article of food.

Oysters, like lobsters, are not good when dead. To ascertain if they are alive, as soon as opened and when one of the shells is removed, touch gently the edge of the oyster, and, if alive, it will contract.

Raw.—When well washed, open them, detaching the upper shell, then detach them from the under shell, but leave them on it; place on a dish, and leave the upper shell on every oyster, and serve thus.

To eat them, you remove the upper shell, sprinkle salt, pepper, and lemon-juice on, and eat.

When raw oysters are served on a table, at which there are gentlemen only, some shallots, chopped fine and gently bruised in a coarse towel, are served with them, on a separate dish. The taste of the shallot agrees very well with that of the oyster.

A Tartar sauce may be served instead of shallots.

To blanch.—Set the oysters and a little water on the fire in a saucepan, take them off at the first boil, skim off the scum from the top, strain them, and drop them in cold water.

The skimming, straining, and dropping in cold water must be done quickly—the quicker the better. If allowed to stay in the warm water, or out of water, they get tough.

In dropping them in cold water, see that they are free from pieces of shell; take them with a fork if necessary.

As soon as in cold water they are ready for use, but they must always be drained again before using them.

When the water used to blanch is employed in preparing them, it is explained in the different receipts.

White wine may be used, instead of water, to blanch them, according to taste.

Fried.—Open the oysters, and put them in a colander for about half an hour. They must be as well drained as possible. Then dip them in egg and roll in bread-crumbs in the following way: Beat one or two, or three, eggs (according to the quantity of oysters to be fried), as for an omelet, turn the oysters into the eggs and stir gently; then take one after another, roll in bread-crumbs; place each one on your left hand, in taking them from the crumbs, and with the other hand press gently on it. Put them away in a cool place for about half an hour, and then dip again in egg, roll in bread-crumbs, and press in the hand as before. It is not indispensable to dip in egg and roll in crumbs a second time; but the oysters are better, and you are well repaid for the little extra work it requires. While you are preparing them, set some fat on the fire in a pan, and when hot enough (*see* Frying) drop the oysters in, stir gently, take off with a skimmer when fried, turn into a colander, add salt, and serve hot.

Roasted.—Place the oysters on a hot stove or range, or on coals, and as soon as they open take off, remove one shell; turn a little melted butter on each, and serve.

There are several other ways.

When blanched, they are served on toast, a little gravy is added, the toast placed on a dessert-plate, and served thus.

Broiled and roasted as above is the same thing.

Oysters scalloped on their own shell, and placed on the range instead of in the oven, are also called broiled.

Scalloped.—Place the oysters when thoroughly washed on a hot stove, and as soon as they open remove one shell, the flatter one of the two, and take them from the fire. Sprinkle salt, pepper, chopped parsley, and bread-crumbs on them; place on each a piece of butter the size of a hazel-nut; put in the oven about ten minutes, and when done add a few drops of meat-gravy, to each, and serve hot.

Another.—Put a quart of oysters and their liquor in a saucepan, set it on the fire, take off at the first boil, and drain. Set a saucepan on the fire with two ounces of butter in it; as soon as melted, add a teaspoonful of flour, stir, and, when turning rather brown, add the juice of the oysters, about a gill of gravy, salt, and pepper; boil gently for about ten minutes, stirring now and then. While it is boiling, place the oysters on scallop-shells, or on silver shells made for that purpose, two or three oysters on each, turn some of the above sauce on each, after it has boiled; dust with bread-crumbs, put a little piece of butter on each shell, and bake for about twelve minutes in a warm oven.

A dozen silver shells served thus make a sightly and excellent dish.

Some truffles, chopped fine, may be added to the sauce, two minutes before taking it from the fire.

Stewed.—Procure two quarts of good and fresh oysters. Set them on a sharp fire, with their liquor and a little water, and blanch as directed. Put four ounces of butter in a saucepan, set on the fire, and when melted stir into it a small tablespoonful of flour; as soon as mixed, add also a teaspoonful of parsley, chopped fine, and about half a pint of broth; boil gently about ten minutes, then add the oysters, salt and pepper, boil again about one minute, dish the whole, sprinkle lemon-juice on, and serve.

An oyster soup is often called a stew.

In Poulette.—In adding chopped mushrooms to the stewed oysters, at the same time that the oysters are put in the pan, you make them in *poulette*.

A la Washington.—Fried oysters are called *à la Washington*, when two, three, or four very large oysters are put together (they adhere very easily), dipped in egg, rolled in bread-crumbs, and fried, as directed above. It is necessary to have a deep pan, and much fat, to immerse them completely.

Pickled oysters are always served as a *hors d'oeuvre*. Place around the oysters some hard-boiled eggs, chopped fine, and serve with oil and vinegar.

Serve them in the same way, with slices of truffles instead of hard-boiled eggs.

They may also be served with lemon-juice only.

Or with shallots chopped fine, and then bruised in a coarse towel. This last one is considered of too strong a taste for ladies.

They are also served with a Tartar sauce.

Scallops.—Blanch the scallops for three minutes, drain them. Put butter on the fire in a frying-pan, and when melted turn the scallops in; stir now and then, take from the fire when fried, add parsley chopped fine, salt, pepper, and serve warm.

On the Shell.—Chop fine a middling-sized onion, and fry it with one ounce of butter. While the onion is frying, chop fine also one quart of scallops and put them with the onion; stir for two or three minutes, or till about half fried, when turn the juice off, put back on the fire, and add one ounce of butter, one gill of white wine, stir for two or three minutes, and if too thick add the juice you have turned off; take from the fire, and mix a yolk of egg with it, add salt, pepper, nutmeg grated, and parsley chopped fine.

Have the scallop shells properly cleaned, or silver shells, spread the mixture on the shells; dust with bread-crumbs, put a piece of butter about the size of a hazel-nut on each, and put in an oven, at about 320 deg. Fahr., for from ten to fifteen minutes.

This is a dish for *breakfast*.

Scallop, scollop, or escalop, are one and the same fish.

CLAMS.

Wash clean with a scrubbing-brush and put them in a kettle; set on a good fire, and leave till they are wide open; then take from the kettle, cut each in two or three pieces, put them in a stewpan with all the water they have disgorged in the kettle, and about four ounces of butter for fifty clams; boil slowly about an hour, take from the fire, and mix with the whole two beaten eggs, and serve warm.

Clams are also eaten raw with vinegar, salt, and pepper.

Chowder.—This popular dish is made in a hundred different ways, but the result is about the same.

It is generally admitted that boatmen prepare it better than others, and the receipts we give below came from the most experienced chowder-men of the Harlem River.

Potatoes and crackers are used in different proportions, the more used, the thicker the chowder will be.

Put in a *pot* (technical name) some small slices of fat salt pork, enough to line the bottom of it; on that, a layer of potatoes, cut in small pieces; on the potatoes, a layer of chopped onions; on the onions, a layer of tomatoes, in slices, or canned tomatoes; on the latter a layer of clams, whole or chopped (they are generally chopped), then a layer of crackers.

Then repeat the process, that is, another layer of potatoes on that of the clams; on this, one of onions, etc., till the pot is nearly full. Every layer is seasoned with salt and pepper. Other spices are sometimes added according to taste; such as thyme, cloves, bay-leaves, and tarragon.

When the whole is in, cover with water, set on a slow fire, and when nearly done, stir gently, finish cooking, and serve.

As we remarked above, the more potatoes that are used, the thicker it will be.

When done, if found too thin, boil a little longer; if found too thick, add a little water, give one boil, and serve.

Another way.—Proceed as above in every particular, except that you omit the clams and crackers, and when the rest is nearly cooked, then add the chopped clams and broken crackers, boil fast about twenty-five minutes longer, and serve.

If found too thick or too thin, proceed exactly as for the one above.

Fish Chowder.—This is made exactly as clam chowder, using fish instead of clams.

Clam Bake.—This is how it is made by the Harlem River clam-baker, TOM RILEY.

Lay the clams on a rock, edge downward, and forming a circle, cover them with fine brush; cover the brush with dry sage; cover the sage with larger brush; set the whole on fire, and when a little more than half burnt (brush and sage), look at the clams by pulling some out, and if done enough, brush the fire, cinders, etc., off; mix some tomato or cauliflower sauce, or catsup, with the clams (minus their shells); add butter and spices to taste, and serve.

Done on sand, the clams, in opening, naturally allow the sand to get in, and it is anything but pleasant for the teeth while eating them.

BEEF.

HOW TO SELECT.

See if the meat is fine, of a clear red color, with yellowish-white fat.

COW BEEF.

Cow beef must also be of a clear red color, but more pale than other beef; the fat is white.

BULL BEEF.

Bull beef is never good; you recognize it when you see hard and yellow fat; the lean part is of a dirty-reddish color.

The rump piece is generally prepared *à la mode*. For steaks, the tenderloin and the piece called the porter-house steak, are the best; rump steaks are seldom tender.

The roasting or baking pieces are the tenderloin, the fillet, and some cuts of the ribs.

For soup, every piece is good; to make rich broth, take pieces of the rump, sucket, round, etc., but every piece makes excellent broth, and therefore excellent soup. (*See* BROTH.)

A good piece of rib, prepared like a fillet or tenderloin, makes an excellent dish, the bones and meat around them being used to make broth.

A LA MODE.

Take from six to twelve pounds of rump and lard it. To lard it you take a steel needle made for that purpose, flat near the pointed end and much larger than an ordinary larding-needle. It must be flat near the point in order to cut the meat so as to make room for the larger part of the needle to pass, and also for the salt pork. This needle is only used for beef *à la mode*.

Cut the salt pork in square strips to fit the needle, (*see* Larding), and proceed.

Examine the piece of beef, lard with the grain of the meat, so that when it is carved the salt pork shall be cut across.

If the piece is too thick to run the strip of pork through, so that both ends stick out, lard one side first then the other. We mean by one side first, this: to be easily handled, the salt pork cannot be cut longer than about four inches; as half an inch of it must stick out of the meat, it leaves only three inches inside, and if the piece of meat be six inches or more thick, of course it would be impossible to have the strip of pork stick out on both sides; therefore, you lard one side first; that is, you run the needle through the meat, leaving the salt pork stick out on the side you commence, and when that side is larded, do the same for the other. You have then the salt pork sticking out on both sides of the meat and looking just as if the strips were running through the whole piece.

Some like more salt pork than others in the beef; the strips may be run thickly or thinly.

Thirty strips may be run into three pounds of meat as well as half a dozen; but about half a pound of salt pork to five pounds of beef is a pretty good proportion.

Then take a saucepan of a proper size for the piece of meat; it must not be too large or too small, but large enough to hold the meat without being obliged to bend or fold it; a crockery pan is certainly the best for that purpose, and one that will go easily in the oven.

Put in the saucepan, for six pounds of beef, half a calf's foot, or a veal-bone if more handy, two ounces of butter, half a handful of parsley (cives, if handy), two bay-leaves, a clove of garlic, a sprig of thyme, two onions, with a clove stuck in each, salt, pepper, half a carrot cut in slices, the rind of the salt pork you have used, and what you may have left of strips; the whole well spread on the bottom of the pan, then the piece of meat over, cover the pan, set on a rather sharp fire and after about ten minutes add half a gill of water; keep the pan covered to the end.

After another ten or fifteen minutes, add about one pint of cold water, turn the meat over, and after about ten minutes more, place the pan in the oven, a rather slow oven (a little above 220 degrees Fahr.), for five or six hours. Dish the meat, skim off the fat on the top of the gravy, give one boil and turn it over the meat and carrots through a strainer.

When the meat is dished; put some carrots *au jus* all around; serve warm.

Cold.—Serve it whole or in slices, with meat jelly, or with a sharp sauce; such as *piquante, ravigote,* etc.

STEWED.

Stewed beef is called also *daube* or *braised* beef, but it is the same.

It may be larded as beef *à la mode,* or not; it may be put whole in the pan or in large dice, according to taste.

The following is for five or six pounds of rump or even a piece of ribs:

Put in a saucepan two ounces of salt pork cut in dice, four sprigs of parsley, two of thyme, two bay-leaves, a clove of garlic, a sprig of sweet basil, two cloves, three carrots cut in pieces, salt, and pepper; put the piece of beef on the whole, wet with a glass of broth, and one of white wine (a liquor-glass of French brandy may also be added); season with six or eight small onions; place in a moderately heated oven, put paste around the cover to keep it air-tight; simmer about six hours; dish the meat with the onions and carrots around it, strain the gravy on the whole, and serve.

Almost any piece of beef may be cooked in the same way, and will be found good, wholesome, and economical.

ROASTED.

How to improve it.—Put the meat in a tureen, with four tablespoonfuls of sweet-oil, salt, pepper, two tablespoonfuls of chopped parsley, four onions cut in slices, two bay-leaves, and the juice of half a lemon; put half of all the above under the meat, and half on it; cover, and leave thus two days in winter, and about eighteen hours in summer.

It certainly improves the meat and makes it more tender. The tenderloin may be improved as well as any other piece.

Then place the meat on the spit before and near a very sharp fire. Baste often with the seasonings, if you have improved the meat; or with a little melted butter, if you have not. Continue basting with what is in the dripping-pan.

Beef must be placed as near the fire as possible, without burning it, however; and then, as soon as a coating or crust is formed all around, remove it by degrees. Remember that the quicker the crust is formed, the more juicy and tender the meat.

Nothing at all is added to form that kind of crust. It is formed by the osmazome of the meat, attracted by the heat, and coming in contact with the air while revolving.

Beef is more juicy when rather underdone; if good, when cut, it has a pinky color inside.

Roast beef may be served with the drippings only, after being strained and the fat removed.

It may also be served in the following ways:

With Potatoes.—Fried potatoes may be served all around the meat, or on a separate dish. Also, potato croquettes.

With Horse-radish.—Grate horse-radish, mix it with the drippings, and serve in a boat.

With a Garniture.—Mix a liver garniture with the gravy, add lemon-juice, place all around the meat, and serve.

With Truffles.—Place the garniture of truffles on and around the meat, turn the drippings on the whole, and serve.

With Tomatoes.—Surround the meat with stuffed tomatoes, strain the gravy on the whole, and serve.

On Purées.—Spread either of the following *purées* on the dish, place the meat over it, strain the drippings on the whole; and serve:

Purées of *asparagus, beans, cauliflowers, celery, Lima beans, onions, green peas, potatoes,* and *mushrooms.*

With Cabbage.—Surround the meat with Brussels cabbages, prepared *au jus*; strain the drippings on the whole, and serve.

With Quenelles.—Place twelve quenelles of chicken around the meat, and serve with the drippings.

TO DECORATE.

When served in any way as described above, one or two or more skewers may be run through craw-fish and a slice of truffle, and stuck in the meat, or through sweetbreads *au jus*, and slices of truffles. It makes a beautiful and good decoration.

The skewers may also be run through chicken-combs, prepared as for *farce*; first through a comb, then through a slice of truffle, through a sweetbread, again through a slice of truffle, then through a craw-fish, and lastly a slice of truffle, or the reverse, according to fancy.

With Rice.—It is surrounded with rice croquettes, the drippings strained over the whole.

We could put down some twenty or more other ways, but any one with an ordinary amount of natural capacity can do it, by varying the *garnitures*, *purées*, *decorations*, etc.

Cold roast-beef is prepared like boiled beef.

BAKED.

Place the meat in a bake-pan, with cold water about a quarter of an inch deep; spread salt, pepper, and a little butter on the meat, cover it with a piece of buttered paper; baste often over the paper, lest it should burn; keep the bottom of the pan covered with juice; if the water and juice are absorbed, add a little cold water and continue basting; turn over two or three times, but keep the paper on the top; if it is burnt, put on another piece. The paper keeps the top of the meat moist, and prevents it from burning or drying.

When done, it is served like roasted beef.

FILLET.

The tenderloin and even the sirloin are sometimes called, or rather known, under the name of fillet, when cooked. It comes from the French *filet*—tenderloin.

Sirloin means surloin; like stock and several others, sirloin is purely English. The surloin is the upper part of the loin, as its prefix indicates; it is *surlonge* in French.

A fillet is generally larded with salt pork by means of a small brass larding-needle; the salt pork cut in strips to fit the needle (*see* LARDING).

If you use a tenderloin, trim off the fat. If it is a piece of ribs, prepared fillet-like, shape it like a fillet as near as possible; the rest is used as directed above.

A piece of ribs is certainly cheaper, and can be had at any time, while the other is as difficult to procure as it is dear.

To lard it.—Have a towel in your left hand and place the meat over it, the most flat and smooth side up, holding it so that the upper part will present a somewhat convex surface, and commence larding at either end and finishing at the other, in this way:

Run the needle through the upper part of the convex surface, commencing at about a quarter of an inch from the edge of one side, running through the meat a distance of about one inch and a half, about half an inch in depth at the middle, and the strip of salt pork sticking out at both ends; that is, where the needle was introduced into the meat, and where it came out of it. Repeat this till you have a row of strips across the meat, the strips being about one-third of an inch apart.

Lard row after row in the same way, and till the whole flat side is covered; the ends of the strips of pork sticking out of each row being intermingled.

To cook it.—It may be roasted or baked exactly in the same way as directed above for roast and baked beef. It may also be improved in the same way.

When cooked in either of the two above ways, it is served with its gravy only, or—

With fried potatoes.
With potato coquettes.
With truffles.
With tomatoes.
With quenelles.
With Madeira-sauce.
With green peas.

The same as roast or baked beef above. It may also be decorated in the same way.

A fillet is also cooked exactly like beef *à la mode*, with the exception that it does not require as long; for a large one, it requires only about three hours.

When cooked thus, it is served with its gravy strained, and decorated with skewers, as above.

With Macaroni.—While the fillet is cooking, prepare a pound of macaroni au jus, and serve the fillet on the macaroni spread on a dish; the gravy of the fillet being mixed with the macaroni when both are done.

Fillet à la Brillat-Savarin.—Cook it in a pan as above, and serve it decorated with sweetbreads and slices of truffles, as described for roast-beef, and with a Champagne-sauce.

A la Chateaubriand.—This is prepared and served like the preceding one, with a *Madeira* instead of a *Champagne* sauce.

Sauté.—When cooked in a pan as directed above, cook mushrooms about ten minutes in the gravy, and serve mushrooms and gravy all around the meat.

A fillet *sauté* is always made with a tenderloin.

As is seen by the above receipts, all the good pieces of beef may be prepared in the ways described, ribs as well as other pieces, and from the plainest to the most *recherché* way, from the cheapest to the most costly manner.

Several names are given to the different ways we have described, such as fillet *financière* (fillet served with a ragout of chicken-combs), fillet Richelieu (fillet with half a dozen skewers), etc.

En Bellevue.—This is the best way to serve it cold. It may be served whole, or part of it, that is, what is left from the preceding dinner. For a supper or lunch, it is the most handy dish, as it can be prepared in advance. Make some meat jelly or calf's-foot jelly, put a thickness of about three-quarters of an inch of it in a tin dish or mould, large enough to hold the fillet; then place on ice to cool, and when congealed and firm enough, place the fillet on it, the larded side downward; fill now with jelly till the fillet is covered, and have a thickness of about three-quarters of an inch above it.

The fillet must not touch the sides of the mould, but be perfectly enveloped in jelly. If the thickness of jelly is even on both sides and all around, it is much more sightly. When the jelly is perfectly congealed and firm, place a dish over the mould, turn upside down, and remove it. Serve as it is.

As a tenderloin is very expensive and rather difficult to get, buy a fine piece of ribs, cut the fleshy part of the shape of a tenderloin, and prepare it as directed above; it makes an excellent and sightly dish. The bony part with the rest of the flesh is used to make broth.

RIBS.

With Vinegar.—Put two tablespoonfuls of fat in a saucepan, and set it on the fire; when melted, put the beef in; say a piece of three pounds, from the round, rump, or rib-piece; brown it on every side; add one gill of vinegar, salt, and a teaspoonful of pepper, cover the pan, and keep on a rather sharp fire for fifteen minutes; then add one carrot and one onion, both sliced, a stalk of thyme, three cloves, two bay-leaves, and six pepper-corns, a pint of broth, and same of water; boil gently till done; dish the meat, strain the sauce over it, and serve.

Ribs may also be broiled like steaks, and served either with a *maître d'hôtel*, mushrooms, potatoes, or water-cress. The low cuts of beef are generally used to make broth, or stewed.

STEAKS.

The best piece of beef for a steak is the tenderloin.

What is called a porter-house steak is the tenderloin, sirloin, and other surrounding parts cut in slices.

A steak should never be less than three-quarters of an inch in thickness.

It should always be broiled; it is inferior in taste and flavor when cooked in a pan (*sauté*), or other utensil, but many persons cook it so, not having the necessary fire or utensil to broil; broiled or *sauté*, it is served alike.

The same rules are applied to steaks of venison, pork, etc.; turtle-steaks are also prepared like beef-steaks.

A good steak does not need any pounding; the object of pounding a steak is to break its fibres. A pounded steak may appear or taste more tender to a person not knowing or never having tasted a good steak, but an experienced palate cannot be deceived.

It is better to broil before than over the fire. (*See* Broiling.)

To cook a steak in an oven or drum, or any other badly-invented machine or contrivance, is not to broil it, but to spoil it.

To make tender.—When cut, trimmed, salted, and peppered, put them in a bowl, and sprinkle some sweet-oil or melted butter over them; turn them over in the bowl every two or three hours for from six to twelve hours.

To cut and prepare.—Cut the meat in round or oval slices, as even as possible, of any size, about one inch in thickness, and trim off the fibres and thin skin that may be around. Do not cut off the fat, but flatten a little each slice with a chopper.

To broil.—when the steaks are cut and prepared as directed, they are slightly greased on both sides with lard or butter (if they have not been in a bowl with oil or butter before cooking them), placed on a warmed gridiron, set before or on a sharp fire, turned over once or twice, and taken off when rather underdone. Salt and pepper them, dish, spread a *maître d'hôtel* over them, and serve very warm.

Cooks and epicures differ about the turning over of steaks; also about broiling them with or without salt; some say that they must not be turned over twice, others are of opinion that they must be turned over two or three, and even more times; some say that they must be salted and peppered before broiling, others say they must not; we have tried the two ways many times, and did not find any difference; if there is any difference at all, it is in the quality of the meat, or in the person's taste, or in the cook's care.

When the steak is served as above, place some fried potatoes all around, and serve hot. Instead of fried potatoes, put some water-cress all around, add a few drops of vinegar, and serve. The water-cress is to be put on raw and cold.

When the steak is dished, spread some anchovy-butter on it instead of a *maître d'hôtel*, and serve warm also. It may also be served with lobster-butter instead of a *maître d'hôtel*. Steaks are also served with horse-radish butter, and surrounded with fried or *soufflé* potatoes.

With a Tomato-Sauce.—Broil and serve the steak as directed above, and serve it with a tomato-sauce instead of a *maître d'hôtel*.

With a Poivrade or Piquante Sauce.—Broil and serve with a *poivrade* or *piquante* sauce, instead of a *maître d'hôtel*.

With Egg.—When the steaks are cut and prepared as directed, dip them in beaten egg, roll them in bread-crumbs, then broil, and serve them with either a *maître d'hôtel* or tomato-sauce, or with potatoes, etc.

With Truffles.—Set a saucepan on the fire with one ounce of butter in it; as soon as melted add half a tablespoonful of flour, stir, and, when turning brown, add also about a gill of broth; stir again for five or six minutes, when mix three or four tablespoonfuls of good gravy with the rest; boil gently ten minutes, take from the fire; slice two or three truffles, mix them with the rest; add salt and pepper to taste; give one boil, turn over the steak which you have broiled as directed, and serve.

With Mushrooms.—Proceed as for truffles in every particular, except that you use mushrooms.

Fancy Steak.—Cut the steak two or three inches thick, butter slightly both sides, lay it on a gridiron well greased and warmed; set it on a moderate fire and broil it well; to cook it through it must be turned over many times, on account of its thickness. Serve like another steak, with a *maître d'hôtel*, *poivrade*, potatoes, or water-cress, etc.

BOILED BEEF.

This is understood to be beef that has been used to make broth—a rump-piece or a rib-piece, boned and tied with twine before cooking it.

a, skewer; *b*, carrot; *c*, turnip; *d*, beef; *e*, carrots and turnips.

With Carrots and Turnips.—Remove the twine, and place the piece of beef on the middle of a dish, with carrots and turnips, cut with a fruit-corer, prepared *au jus* or glazed, and arranged all around it; also, some skewers run through pieces of carrot and turnip, and then stuck in the piece of beef. (See cut p. 174.) Serve warm.

With Brussels Cabbage, or Sprouts.—Serve the beef as above, surrounded with sprouts *au jus*, and also ornamented with skewers run through sprouts, with a piece of turnip between each.

In Bourgeoise.—Serve the piece of beef warm, decorated if handy, and surrounded with fried potatoes cut with a vegetable spoon or in fillets, and gravy spread over the whole.

If not decorated, a few sprigs of parsley may be spread on the beef.

With Onions.—Serve the beef as above, and surround it with glazed onions.

With Celery.—When served as above, the meat is surrounded with a *purée* of celery.

With Cauliflowers.—Serve warm, with a garniture of cauliflowers all around. It may be decorated with skewers.

With Chestnuts.—Glaze chestnuts as for dessert; run the skewers through a chestnut first, then through a fried potato, and then through a slice of carrot, and stick one at each end of the piece of beef; put chestnuts all around, spread some gravy over the whole, and serve warm.

In Croquettes.—Proceed as for *croquettes* of chicken.

Hollandaise.—Cut the meat in fillets and put it in a saucepan, with about two ounces of fat or butter to a pound of meat; set on the fire and stir for ten minutes. Then add a tablespoonful of flour and stir about one minute, with warm water enough to half cover the meat, and boil about five minutes, stirring now and then.

Mix together in a bowl two yolks of eggs, the juice of half a lemon, and two or three tablespoonfuls of the sauce from the saucepan in which the beef is; turn the mixture into the saucepan, stir and mix, add salt and pepper to taste, give one boil, and serve warm.

Broiled.—Cut the meat in slices about one inch in thickness, broil, and serve like steaks.

Au Gratin.—Put two ounces of butter in a saucepan on the fire, and when melted sprinkle into it two tablespoonfuls of bread-crumbs, two or three mushrooms chopped, a teaspoonful of chopped onions, same of parsley, a pinch of allspice, salt, and pepper; stir for about two minutes, add a little broth to make the whole rather liquid. Cut one pound of boiled beef in slices, place them in a tin or silver dish, turn the mixture over them, dust with bread-crumbs; put half a dozen pieces of butter here and there on the top, and bake for about fifteen minutes.

Take from the oven when done, add a few drops of lemon juice all over, and serve warm in the dish in which it was baked.

With a *maître d'hôtel, piquante, Mayonnaise, Robert, ravigote, Tartar,* or *tomato* sauce.

Cut it in slices, place them on a dish, spread on them some chopped parsley and slices of pickled cucumbers, and send thus to the table, with either of the above sauces in a saucer to be used with it.

IN MIROTON.

Put a piece of butter the size of an egg in a stewpan (this is for about two pounds), and set it on the fire; when melted, put in it four middling-sized onions, cut in slices when nearly cooked, sprinkle on them a pinch of flour, and stir till it takes a golden color; then add half a glass of white wine, and as much of broth, also salt, pepper, and a little grated nutmeg; boil until well cooked, and till the sauce is reduced; then add the boiled beef, cut in slices, and leave it fifteen minutes; dish it, pour on a few drops of vinegar, and serve.

Hushed.—Proceed exactly as for *miroton*, except that the beef is cut in strips or chopped, and that no wine is used.

IN SALAD.

Cut it in very thin and short slices, and place them on a dish with chopped parsley; put in a saucer sweet-oil and vinegar, according to the quantity of beef you have, two tablespoonfuls of oil to one of vinegar, salt, pepper, and some mustard; beat the whole a little, pour on the slices, and serve.

CORNED BEEF.

Corned beef is generally boiled. Soak the corned beef in cold water for some time, according to how salt it is.

Set it on the fire, covered with cold water, and boil gently till done.

With Cabbage.—Blanch the cabbage for about five minutes, and drain. Then put it to cook with the corned beef when the latter is about half done; serve both on the same dish, or separately, according to taste.

Corned beef, when boiled as above, without cabbage, can be served and decorated, in every way, like boiled beef. It certainly makes sightly as well as good dishes for a family dinner.

A piece of corned beef, surrounded with a garniture as we have described above, decorated with skewers, is very often served as a *relevé* at an extra dinner.

Cold Corned Beef.—A whole piece, or part of it, may be served *en Bellevue*, the same as a *fillet en Bellevue*; it is also excellent.

TONGUE.

Clean and blanch it for about ten minutes—till the white skin can be easily removed. After ten minutes boiling, try if it comes off; if not, boil a little longer, then skin it well.

To boil.—When skinned, put it in your soup-kettle with the beef, etc., to make broth, and leave it till done. When boiled, the tongue may be served and decorated exactly the same as boiled beef, in every way.

Stewed.—Cut square fillets of bacon, which dredge in a mixture of chopped parsley, cives, salt, pepper, and a little allspice; lard the tongue with the fillets. Put in a crockery stewpan two ounces of bacon cut in dice, four sprigs of parsley, two of thyme, one of sweet basil, two bay-leaves, a clove of garlic, two cloves, two carrots cut in pieces, four small onions, salt, and pepper; lay the tongue on the whole, wet with half a glass of white wine and a glass of broth; set on a moderate fire, and simmer about five hours—keep it well covered; then put the tongue on a dish, strain the sauce on it, and serve. It is a delicious dish.

It may also be served with vegetables around, or with tomato-sauce.

Another way.—When prepared as above directed, put it on the fire with the same seasonings as the preceding one; simmer four hours and take from the fire; put the tongue on a dish and let it cool, then place it on the spit before a good fire, and finish the cooking; serve it warm with an oil, or *piquante* sauce.

If any is left of either of the two, put in a pan the next day, wet with a little broth, set on the fire, and when warm serve it on a *purée*; do not allow it to boil.

BRAIN.

Soak it in lukewarm water and clean well, so as to have it free from blood, fibres, and thin skin; then soak it again in cold water for twelve hours in winter and six in summer. Put in a crockery stewpan one ounce of bacon cut in slices, one carrot cut in pieces, two sprigs of parsley, one of thyme, a bay-leaf, a clove, four small onions cut in slices, a teaspoonful of chopped cives, salt, pepper, a pint of white wine, as much of broth, and then the brain; set on a moderate fire for half an hour and take it off; dish the brain and place it in a warm place; then strain the sauce, put it back on the fire with the brain in it, add two or three mushrooms cut in pieces, leave on the fire from ten to fifteen minutes, and serve it, parted in two, with fried parsley around.

Another way.—When the brain is cleaned and prepared as above, cut it in eight pieces. Mix well together a little flour, chopped parsley and cives, also a pinch of allspice; roll the pieces of brain in it, so as to allow the mixture to adhere to them; have some butter in a frying-pan on the fire, and when hot put the pieces of brain in it; fry gently, and serve with fried parsley around.

HEART.

Soak it in lukewarm water for two hours, free it from blood and skin, drain and wipe dry; then stuff it with sausage-meat, to which you have added three or four onions chopped fine, put it in a rather quick oven, or on the spit before a good fire (if on the spit, envelop it with buttered paper), basting from time to time; it takes about an hour and a half to cook a middling-sized one; serve it with a *vinaigrette, piquante, poivrade,* or *ravigote* sauce.

It may also be fried with butter, and cut in slices, but it is not as good as in the above way; it generally becomes hard in frying.

KIDNEYS.

First split the kidneys in four pieces, trim off as carefully as possible the sinews and fat that are inside, then cut in small pieces.

Sauté.—The quicker this is done the better the kidney. For a whole one put about two ounces of butter in a frying-pan and set it on a very sharp fire, toss it round so as to melt the butter as fast as possible, but without allowing it to blacken; as soon as melted, turn the cut kidney in, stir now and then with a wooden spoon for about three minutes, then add a tablespoonful of flour, stir again the same as before for about one minute, when add a gill of white wine and about one of broth; stir again now and then till the kidney is rather underdone, and serve immediately.

If the kidney is allowed to boil till perfectly done, it will very seldom be tender.

It may be done with water instead of wine and broth; in that case, add a few drops of lemon-juice just before serving it.

Prepare and serve it also as calf's-kidney, in every way as directed for the same.

LIVER.

Cut the liver in slices a quarter of an inch in thickness, sprinkle on them salt and pepper, place them on a gridiron, and set on a sharp fire; turn over only once, and serve rather underdone, with butter and chopped parsley, kneaded together and spread between the slices.

A few drops of lemon-juice may be added.

Another way.—When the liver is cut in slices, as above, put a piece of butter in a frying-pan on the fire, and when melted, lay the slices in; turn over only once, then serve, with salt, pepper, vinegar, and chopped parsley.

TAIL.

Cut the tail at the joint, so as to make as many pieces as there are joints; throw the pieces in boiling water for fifteen minutes, and drain them. When cold and dry, put them in a saucepan with a bay-leaf, two onions, with a clove stuck in each, two sprigs of parsley, and one of thyme, a clove of garlic, salt, pepper, half a wine-glass of white wine, and a few thin slices of salt pork; cover with broth or water, and set on a moderate fire for two hours. Dish the pieces, strain the sauce on them, and serve with a garniture of cabbage, or with any *purée*.

TRIPE.

How to clean and prepare.—Scrape and wash it well several times in boiling water, changing the water every time, then put in very cold water for about twelve hours, changing the water two or three times; place it in a pan, cover it with cold water; season with parsley, cives, onions, one or two cloves of garlic, cloves, salt, and pepper; boil gently five hours, take out and drain.

In case the water should boil away, add more.

You may save all the trouble of cleaning and preparing, by buying it ready prepared, as it is generally sold in cities.

Broiled.—When prepared, dip it in lukewarm butter, roll in bread-crumbs, place on a gridiron, and set it on a moderate fire; turn over as many times as is necessary to broil it well, and serve with a *vinaigrette, piquante,* or Tartar sauce; also with a tomato-sauce.

Stewed.—Put in a stewpan two ounces of salt pork, cut in dice, three carrots cut in slices, eight small onions, four cloves, two bay-leaves, two cloves of garlic, a piece of nutmeg, four sprigs of parsley, two of thyme, a dozen stalks of cives, six pepper-corns, the fourth part of an ox-foot cut in four pieces, salt, pepper, about two ounces of ham cut in dice, then three pounds of double tripe on the whole; spread two ounces of fat bacon cut in thin slices on the top; wet with half white wine and half water, or water only if you choose; put the cover on, and if not air-tight, put some paste around; set in a slow oven for six hours, then take the tripe out, strain the sauce, skim off the fat when cool, then put the sauce and tripe again in your pan, warm well, and serve in crockery plates or bowls placed on chafing-dishes, as it is necessary to keep it warm while eating. It is good with water only, but better with half wine. This is also called *à la mode de Caen.*

In Poulette.—When cleaned and prepared as directed, cut one pound of tripe in strips about one and a half inches broad, then cut again contrariwise, so as to make small fillets. Put one ounce of butter in a saucepan with half a tablespoonful of flour, and mix cold; add two gills of water, mix again, set on the fire, stir now and then, give one boil, put the tripe in, salt and pepper to taste; boil two minutes and dish the whole; put a teaspoonful of chopped parsley all over, and serve hot.

Aux Fines Herbes.—Broil the tripe, and serve it with sauce *fines herbes.*

Tripe may be bought pickled; it is then served at breakfast and lunch.

SMOKED BEEF'S TONGUE.

Soak the smoked tongue in cold water for at least three hours, change the water once or twice during the process. Then take off the thin skin or strip around if there is any; put the tongue in a saucepan with two sprigs of thyme, two of parsley, a bay-leaf, two cloves, six small onions, and a clove of garlic; fill the pan with cold water, and let simmer about six hours. If the water is boiling away, add more. Take from the fire, let cool as it is, then take it out of the water; clean it, let dry, and serve it when cold.

Cut the tongue, when prepared as above, either in slices or in strips, and use for sandwiches, or serve it whole, with a cucumber, *piquante*, *poivrade*, or tomato sauce, at breakfast or lunch. It may also be served in *vinaigrette*.

When prepared as directed above, serve it as a fillet of beef *en Bellevue*, for supper, lunch, or breakfast. It makes a fine and delicious dish.

It is used also to stuff boned turkeys and other birds, as directed in those receipts; always boil it as directed above, before using it.

When served with any of the above sauces, it may be decorated with skewers the same as boiled beef.

Larded.—When boiled, lard it with salt pork, and bake it for about one hour in a moderately heated oven, and serve it with the same sauces as above.

Cut in slices and served with parsley, it is a *hors-d'oeuvre*.

MUTTON.

HOW TO SELECT.

You may be sure that mutton is good when the flesh is rather black, and the fat white; if the fat breaks easily, it is young.

The wether is much superior to the ewe.

You will know if a leg of mutton comes from a wether, if there is a large and hard piece of fat on one side at the larger and upper end; if from a ewe, that part is merely a kind of skin, with a little fat on it.

ROASTED.

A piece of mutton to roast must not be too fresh, it is much more tender when the meat is rather seasoned, but not tainted, or what is sometimes called "high." When on the spit, place it near the fire, baste immediately with a little melted butter, and then with the drippings. As soon as you notice that a kind of crust or coating has formed around the piece of meat, remove it a little from the fire by degrees; and continue basting till done. The quicker the crust is formed, though without burning the meat, the more juicy and tender it will be.

Roast mutton, like roast beef, is better served rather underdone, but should be a little more done than beef. When properly roasted, the meat, whatever piece it may be, either a loin or saddle, a leg, shoulder, or a breast, may be served with its gravy only; that is, with what is in the dripping-pan after having removed all the fat, also on a *soubise* or on a *purée* of sorrel. The above pieces may also be served in the following ways:

With Potatoes.—When dished, surround the meat with potatoes, either fried, mashed, or in *croquettes*.

With Quenelles.—Dish the meat, place half a dozen *quenelles* around it, and decorate it with skewers which you have run through a *quenelle* and then through a craw-fish and stuck in the meat.

With Carrots.—When dished, put all around the meat carrots *au jus*, or glazed and cut with a vegetable spoon.

With Spinach.—Spinach *au jus* when done is spread on the dish, the meat is put on it, and served warm. Do the same with a *purée* of cauliflowers.

BAKED.

All the above pieces are baked as well as roasted; and when done, served exactly in the same and every way as when roasted.

Put the meat in a baking-pan with a little butter spread over it; cover the bottom of the pan with cold water, then put in a quick oven. After it has been in the oven for about fifteen minutes, baste and place a piece of buttered paper on the top of the meat. If the bottom of the pan is getting dry, add a little more water, but it is seldom the case except with inferior meat. When you see rather too much fat in the pan, take from the oven, turn the fat off, put cold water instead, and put back in the oven to finish the cooking. If the paper burns, put on another piece; but by basting often over the paper, it will remain pretty long before burning.

With a small knife or a skewer you ascertain when done enough or to your liking; never cook by guess or by hearsay; the oven may be quicker one day than another, or slower; the meat may be more tender, or more hard; remember that if you cook by guess (we mean, to put down, as a matter of course, that it takes so many hours, or so many minutes, to bake this or that), and stick to it, you will fail nine times out of ten. When done, serve as directed above.

In Croquettes.—Make and serve as chicken *croquettes*.

In Haricot or Ragout.—Take a neck or breast piece of mutton, which cut in pieces about two inches long and one broad. Put them in a saucepan (say three pounds) with two ounces of butter, set on the fire and stir occasionally till turning rather brown, then add a tablespoonful of flour, stir for one minute, cover with cold water, add one onion whole, salt, a bunch of seasonings composed of four sprigs of parsley, one of thyme, a bay-leaf, and a clove, one clove of garlic, chopped fine. Boil gently till about two-thirds done, stirring now and then; add potatoes, peeled, quartered, and cut, as far as possible, of the shape of a carpel of orange. The proportion is, about as many pieces of potatoes as of meat. Boil again gently till done, place the pieces of meat in the middle of the dish, the potatoes around, the juice or sauce over the whole, and serve. Skim off the fat, if any, before turning the sauce over the rest.

BREAST BOILED.

Put the breast entire in a saucepan, with a sprig of thyme, two of parsley, a bay-leaf, a clove, salt, and pepper, cover with water, set on the fire, boil gently till cooked, and then drain. Put in a frying-pan three tablespoonfuls of sweet-oil, a teaspoonful of chopped parsley, salt, and pepper; when hot lay the breast in and fry it all around for five minutes; then take it off, roll it in bread-crumbs, place it on a gridiron, and set on a good fire for five minutes; turn it over once only, then serve it with a *piquante, poivrade,* or tomato sauce. It may also be served on a *purée* of sorrel.

NECK BROILED.

Prepare and serve exactly the same as a breast broiled.

A breast or a neck piece broiled may be served on a *soubise*. It may also be served with a *maître d'hôtel* or mushroom sauce, also with a *piquante* or any other sharp sauce.

CHOPS.

Broiled.—Trim and flatten the chops with a chopper, sprinkle salt and pepper on both sides, dip them in melted butter, place them on a gridiron, and set on a sharp fire, turn over two or three times to broil properly, and when done, serve them around a dish, one lapping over the other, etc., and serve with the gravy. It takes about twelve minutes to cook with a good fire.

Another way.—When trimmed and flattened, dip them in beaten egg, roll them in bread-crumbs and broil, either as they are, or enveloped in buttered paper, and serve them with a *maître d'hôtel* sauce.

Sautés.—When trimmed and flattened, fry them with a little butter on both sides; then take the chops from the pan and put them in a warm place. Leave in the pan only a tablespoonful of fat, add to it three times as much broth, a teaspoonful of parsley and green onions, two shallots, two pickled cucumbers, all chopped fine, and a pinch of allspice; give one boil, pour the whole on the chops, also the juice of half a lemon, and serve.

The same, with Vegetables.—Put in a frying-pan a piece of butter the size of two walnuts for four chops, set on a good fire, and when hot lay the chops in, after having flattened them with a chopper, and having sprinkled salt and pepper on both sides; add a clove, and a teaspoonful of chopped parsley and green onions; leave thus five minutes, turn over once or twice; then add also half a wine-glass of broth, same of white wine, and finish the cooking. Take the chops off the pan and put them in a warm place. Boil the sauce in the pan ten minutes, turn it on the chops, put a garniture of vegetables around, and serve. Throw away the clove just before serving.

Another way.—Have a piece of butter the size of an egg for eight chops in a crockery vessel, and set it on a good fire; when melted take from the fire, lay the chops in, after having flattened them; then cover them with a sheet of buttered paper; place the vessel in a rather hot oven, and when cooked serve them on a *maître d'hôtel, provençale,* or tomato sauce. They may also be served on a *purée* of sorrel, or one of potatoes.

The same, in Papillote.—Cut the chops rather thin, beat them gently and flatten them; then proceed as for veal cutlets in *papillotes* in every particular.

Financière.—Broil the chops, either with or without egg and crumbs, and serve them with a *financière* garniture.

Soubise.—The chops are either broiled or fried; either broiled only dipped in lukewarm butter or in beaten egg and crumbs and then served on a *soubise.* A little lemon-juice may be added when they are on the dish.

Jardinière.—Cut two carrots and two turnips with a vegetable spoon and set on the fire with cold water and salt; boil gently till tender, and drain. Boil also in the same way, in another pan and till tender, two tablespoonfuls of green peas, or string-beans cut in pieces, and drain also. Then put carrots, turnips, peas, or beans, back on the fire, in the same pan with a little gravy and broth, enough to cover them, salt, and pepper; boil gently five minutes; then put the chops in after being fried as directed below; boil another five minutes; take from the fire, place the chops around the dish, one lapping over the other, and so that an empty place is left in the middle; turn the carrots, turnips, and peas, with the sauce in that empty place, and serve. Salt and pepper the chops on both sides; fry them in a little butter till about three-quarters done; then take off and put with the vegetables as directed above. They may be broiled instead of fried, which is better.

A la Princesse.—Trim the chops as usual and salt and pepper both sides. Chop very fine a piece of lean veal about half a pound for six or eight chops, according to size, then pound it and mix it with half a teaspoonful of flour, a pinch of nutmeg, salt, pepper, a yolk of egg, two tablespoonfuls of bread-crumbs and one ounce of butter. If too firm the butter must be melted so as to mix better. Put the mixture in a saucepan, set on a good fire, stir for ten minutes, and take off. Then grease the paste-board slightly with butter, put a teaspoonful of the mixture here and there on it, roll and make small balls of it, drop them in boiling broth or water, boiling about fifteen minutes, and take off with a skimmer. Dip the chops in melted butter, then in beaten eggs, and roll in bread-crumbs; fry them with a little butter. Fry the balls also. Place the chops on the dish, the bones toward the edge, and the balls between the chops; serve warm. A few balls may be placed in the middle.

With Mushrooms.—Broil and serve them with a *purée* of mushrooms, or with a mushroom garniture.

Mutton chops, broiled, may be served with every kind of butter, every garniture, and every sauce, according to taste; they may also be served with every *purée*.

A French cook once said he could serve mutton *chops* in three hundred ways, *apples* in two hundred ways, and *eggs* in four hundred ways. The culinary science and art is advanced enough to-day to double the above figures, and have plenty to spare.

LEG.

Besides being prepared as directed for roast mutton, a leg of mutton, roasted or baked, may be served in the following ways:

Boil white beans and drain them as directed, then put them on the fire with the drippings of the leg of mutton for ten minutes, stirring now and then, and serve them with it. They may also be kept in the dripping-pan for ten minutes, when boiled and drained, before the leg is done. If the leg of mutton is baked, set them on the fire for about ten minutes, with the gravy, stirring occasionally. Serve either on the same or on a separate dish.

With Currant Jelly.—Roast or bake the leg of mutton, and serve it with currant jelly or with a *purée.*

Provençale.—With a sharp-pointed knife, make a small cut in the leg of mutton here and there, and large enough to stick into the cut a clove of garlic. Make as many cuts as you please, from six to twenty, according to taste, and in each cut stick a clove of garlic. When prepared thus, roast or bake, and serve it with either of the following sauces: *piquante, poivrade, ravigote, rémolade,* Robert, shallot, Tartar, tomato, and in *vinaigrette.*

Decorated.—A leg of mutton may be decorated the same as a fillet of beef.

Stewed.—Take the large bone out, leaving the bone at the smaller end as a handle; cut off also the bone below the knuckle, and fix it with skewers; then put it in a stewpan with a pinch of allspice, four onions, two cloves, two carrots cut in four pieces each, a small bunch of parsley, two bay-leaves, three sprigs of thyme, salt, pepper, two ounces of bacon cut in slices, a quarter of a pint of broth, and water enough just to cover it; set on a good fire, and after one hour of boiling add a liquor-glass of French brandy. Let simmer then for about five hours, in all about six hours; then dish it, strain the sauce on it, and serve.

We would advise those who have never tasted of a leg of mutton cooked as above, to try it.

It may be served also with white beans cooked in water and fried in butter, or on fried potatoes.

The next day.—If you have a piece left for the next day, cut it in thin slices after dinner, place the slices on a dish, with parsley under, in the middle, and above, and keep in a cold place.

A while before dinner you put in a stewpan a piece of butter (the quantity to be according to the quantity of meat), and set it on a good fire; when melted, sprinkle in, gradually, a little flour, stirring with a wooden spoon; when of a proper thickness, and of a brownish color, add a glass of broth, salt, pepper, a few pickled cucumbers cut in slices, and two or three mushrooms; boil ten minutes; lay the slices of meat in, subdue the fire, simmer twenty minutes, and serve.

The same, in another way.—Chop fine the slices of leg of mutton, put a piece of butter in a stewpan, and set it on the fire; when melted, place the chopped meat in, keep stirring with a wooden spoon for about ten minutes; then add two or three tablespoonfuls of broth, salt, pepper, and a pinch of allspice; simmer fifteen minutes, and serve with fried eggs all around the dish.

Boiled.—Set a saucepan on the fire with cold water enough to cover the leg of mutton, add salt; at the first boil put the leg of mutton in, wrapped up in a towel. Boil gently till done. For a middling-sized one, it takes about two hours. Remove the towel, dish the leg of mutton, spread a caper-sauce over it, and serve hot. The sauce may also be served in a boat or saucer.

Cold.—What is left of it may be prepared like cold mutton in vinaigrette.

SHOULDER.

Shoulder boned.—Split the shoulder just in the middle, on the inside, lengthwise and following the middle of the bones; remove the flat bone at the larger end first. This is easily done by scraping the meat off the bone on both sides, and then pulling it off. Do the same with the remaining bone. Spread the shoulder open on the table, the inside up, salt and pepper it, then spread on it the same stuffing as for a chicken stuffed with sausage-meat. Roll the shoulder round, tie it with twine, and roast or bake it. When roasted or baked, serve with the gravy.

On a Purée.—Bone and roll the shoulder as above directed, but do not stuff it; roast or bake it, and serve it on a *purée* of potatoes, beans, peas, lentils, or any other vegetable; place the shoulder in the middle of a dish, cut it in slices, and place them all around the *purée*, one lapping over the other; turn the gravy over the whole through a strainer, and serve hot.

With a Sauce.—When baked or roasted as above, with or without stuffing, serve it with a *piquante, ravigote,* or *Robert* sauce.

Boiled.—Boil, and serve it with a caper-sauce, the same as the leg.

SADDLE.

Prepare, cook, and serve the saddle in the same way as the leg—roasted or baked, warm or cold.

COLD MUTTON.

Served cold, à la Vinaigrette.—A shoulder of mutton, roasted or baked, after being boned, makes a handsome dish served cold. Cut any piece of cold mutton that you may have, in thin slices, as evenly as possible. Place a paste-cutter, about an inch and a half in diameter, in the middle of an oval dish; then place the slices of meat all around the dish, one slice lapping over another; the dish being oval, the slices of meat will touch the paste-cutter on two sides, but there will be two empty places on the two other sides, which you fill with hard-boiled white of egg chopped fine, and hard-boiled yolk of egg chopped fine also; they must not be mixed, and the yolk must be farther from the paste-cutter, the white touching it. Put a string of chopped yolk of egg all around the meat, and outside of it one of chopped white of egg around the yolk, and one of chopped parsley around the white. Remove the paste-cutter, and put a rose, or two or three pinks, in its place, or a small bunch of violets. Place one or three capers on each small heap of yolk of egg that is on the middle of the dish, and also some capers here and there on the string of white of egg.

Place a rose at each end of the dish, as indicated in the cut opposite; six radishes around the dish, also as indicated in the cut, and you have a dish as sightly as can be made, and an excellent one, too. Serve with the following sauce in a boat or saucer: Put in a bowl half a teaspoonful of mustard, a little pepper and salt; then pour one or two tablespoonfuls of vinegar on, little by little, beating with a fork at the same time; again, three or four tablespoonfuls of oil, and in the same way; and when the whole is well mixed, serve.

A, two roses, one at each end; B, six radishes around; C, slices of meat; D, eggs; E, yolks of eggs; F, parsley.

SHEEP'S BRAIN.

Prepare, cook, and serve as calf's brain.

FEET.

Broiled.—Throw them in boiling water for ten minutes, clean and scrape off the hair and take out the large bone. Put in a saucepan a bay-leaf, one clove, a tablespoonful of vinegar, a clove of garlic, two sprigs of parsley, two green onions, salt, pepper, a piece of butter the size of two walnuts, half a pint of broth, then a dozen feet on the whole; set on a slow fire, simmer one hour, stir now and then, take from the fire and let cool. Then dip each foot in beaten egg, and roll it in bread-crumbs; place them on a gridiron; turn over to broil both sides properly, and serve them with the sauce in which they have been cooked, after having strained it. They may also be served on a *piquante, poivrade, ravigote,* or *Robert* sauce.

In Poulette.—Prepare and clean them as directed above. Put in a saucepan four ounces of salt pork cut in dice, two ounces of lard, salt, and white pepper; when warm, add three sprigs of parsley, two of thyme, a bay-leaf, one clove, four onions, and one carrot, cut in slices, a quarter of a lemon, also cut in slices, free from rind and seed, two tablespoonfuls of flour; this last must be added by sprinkling it little by little, stirring the while with a wooden spoon; five minutes after, place the feet in, cover the whole with warm water, and let simmer gently for five or six hours. After that time see if the meat can be easily detached from the bones, and if so, they are cooked; if not, leave them a little longer, and take from the fire as soon as it is easily detached, but do not detach it. Put in a stewpan a piece of butter the size of two walnuts; when melted, sprinkle in it a tablespoonful of flour, stir with a wooden spoon, then put the feet in, add a teaspoonful of chopped parsley and green onions, a little piece of nutmeg, salt, pepper, and two or three mushrooms cut in slices or pieces; wet with broth; simmer half an hour, take from the fire, and throw away the piece of nutmeg; mix with the whole two yolks of eggs well beaten and a tablespoonful of vinegar, and serve.

SHEEP'S KIDNEYS, BROILED.

Split them in two, and put them in cold water for five minutes; trim off the pellicle or thin skin, run a skewer through, sprinkle salt and pepper on, place them on the gridiron, and set on a good fire; turn over, and when broiled, serve them with a piece of butter and chopped parsley kneaded together, and placed on each kidney; add also a few drops of lemon-juice.

You may also, when broiled, serve them on a *maître d'hôtel* sauce.

The same, in Brochette.—Proceed as above in every particular, except that you place the kidneys on the spit instead of on the gridiron. Serve them in the same way.

The same, with Champagne.—Cut the kidneys in slices, each in ten or twelve pieces. Put in a stewpan a piece of butter the size of two walnuts, and set it on the fire; when melted, add a teaspoonful of chopped parsley, same of mushrooms, a pinch of grated nutmeg, salt, pepper, and the kidneys; keep tossing till they become stiff, then sprinkle on them a saltspoonful of flour, stirring with a wooden spoon the while; add also a wine-glass of Champagne, or of good white wine; subdue the fire, and let simmer till cooked; take from the fire, add about one ounce of fresh butter, and the juice of half a lemon, and serve. This is a very delicate dish.

SHEEP'S TAILS.

Put in a stewpan two ounces of bacon cut in slices, with a bay-leaf, two sprigs of parsley, one of thyme, one clove, six small onions, one carrot cut in four pieces, then about six tails; cover the whole with broth and white wine, half of each; add salt and pepper. Place the pan in a moderately heated oven; it will take about four hours to cook them. After that time, take the tails from the pan, and put them in a warm place, then strain the sauce in which they have cooked, skim off the fat if too much of it, put the sauce back in the pan, and set on the fire; let it reduce till rather thick, place the tails on a *purée*, turn the sauce on them, and serve.

SHEEP'S TONGUES.

Soak the tongues in cold water for two hours in winter, and one in summer, and drain. Throw them in boiling water, and leave till you can easily take the skin off; then skin and clean well, split in two lengthwise, and let cool. Put in a stewpan two ounces of bacon cut in thin slices, a bay-leaf, two sprigs of thyme, four of parsley, two cloves, three green onions and six small red or white ones, one carrot cut in four pieces, salt and pepper, then the tongues; add also half a pint of broth, same of water, same of white wine; set in a moderately heated oven, and simmer about four hours; have the stewpan covered as nearly air-tight as possible. Then take the tongues from the pan and drain them; knead well together two ounces of fresh butter, with two teaspoonfuls of chopped parsley, a little salt and allspice; spread some on each of the tongues as soon as they are cold; envelop each in oiled paper, broil them gently on a slow fire, and serve with the paper.

You may also when prepared and cooked as above directed, and instead of broiling them, place a *purée* on a dish, and serve them on a *purée*, pouring on the whole the sauce in which they have cooked, and straining it at the same time.

They are really more delicate when broiled.

LAMB.

To select.—The flesh must be like that of mutton, rather black, and the fat white.

There is no difference in the wether and ewe. The shorter the quarters are the better the meat, and the fore as well as the hind quarter. With the exception that the breast-piece is prepared also in *épigramme*, and that it is cut in quarters instead of dividing it like mutton, lamb may be prepared in the same and every way like mutton. The quarters may be prepared like shoulder, leg, and saddle of mutton.

Chops may be cut and prepared the same as mutton-chops.

Fore-Quarter.—According to the opinion of a great many epicures, the fore-quarter is the best part of the lamb; but, as we have previously said, every one to his liking.

Lard it slightly, and envelop it with buttered paper, place it upon the spit before a good fire; when done take from the fire, and take the paper off, sprinkle on it salt, pepper, and chopped parsley; put back on the spit before a sharp fire, just long enough to allow it to take a fine color; then take off, run a knife under the shoulder to make a small hole, pour *maître d'hôtel* sauce in it, and serve either as it is, with its gravy, or on a *purée* of sorrel.

To bake it.—Put it in a baking-pan, spread a little salt, pepper, and butter over it; cover it with a piece of buttered paper; have the bottom of the pan covered with cold water and put in a warm oven, baste often till done. If the paper burns, put on another piece. Run a small knife or a skewer into the meat, to ascertain when properly done.

It may be served with the gravy only, after having removed the fat, or with a *piquante, poivrade*, or *maître d'hôtel* sauce.

It is also served with a garniture of mushrooms or onions, or with a *macédoine,* or on a *purée* of spinach, or of sorrel.

Hind-Quarter.—Throw it in boiling water for five minutes, and drain. Put in a stewpan a piece of butter the size of an egg, and set on the fire; when melted, mix in it a tablespoonful of flour; after which, pour in, little by little, a pint and a half of boiling water, stirring with a wooden spoon all the time; then put the meat in the pan, add four onions, a bay-leaf, two cloves, three sprigs of parsley, two of thyme, salt, and pepper; about fifteen minutes before it is done, add two or three mushrooms cut in slices, take from the fire when cooked, place the meat on a dish with the mushrooms and onions around, or if preferred, without either; strain the sauce on the meat, and serve.

If the sauce is not thick enough, mix the yolk of an egg in it just before serving.

Roasted.—Roast and serve the hind-quarter in the same way as directed for the fore-quarter.

Baked.—Bake and serve it also in the same and every way like the fore-quarter.

Epigramme.—Put a breast of lamb in a saucepan, cover it with cold water, season with a small onion and one clove stuck in it, two stalks of parsley, a piece of carrot, one of turnip, and salt. Boil gently till you can pull off the bones easily. It may also be boiled in the soup-kettle while making broth. When the bones come off easily, take from the fire, pull out all the small bones and cut out the large one. Place the breast in a large bakepan, with some weight over so as to flatten it, and leave it so till perfectly cold. Then cut it in pieces of rhombic shape about four inches long and two inches broad; salt and pepper each piece on both sides; dip them in beaten egg, roll in bread-crumbs and fry them with a little butter, and serve on a tomato, *piquante*, *ravigote*, or *soubise* sauce, or on any *purée*.

When the sauce is spread on the dish, place the pieces of lamb all around it, one lapping over the other, and forming a kind of oblong string, and serve warm.

Another.—When the *épigramme* is prepared as above and ready to be served, have as many mutton-chops as you have pieces of meat from the breast; dish in the same way, except that you put one piece of the breast and then a mutton-chop fried in the same way as the pieces of meat; the chops lapping over the pieces of breast, and *vice versa*.

Broiled.—The same may be broiled instead of fried, and served in the same way.

Roasted entire.—Skewer a lamb properly on the spit, envelop it with buttered paper, place before a good fire, baste often with melted butter first, and then with the drippings; when nearly done take the paper off, let the lamb take a fine color around, and serve it with the gravy. It may be served with a garniture around and decorated with skewers, the same as directed for fillet of beef; it then makes a sightly as well as a delicious dish.

Served with a garniture and decorated as directed for a fillet of beef, it is served as a *relevé* at a grand dinner, and as an *entrée* at a family dinner.

Cold.—Cold lamb is served in every way like cold mutton. A part left from a roasted piece may be enveloped in buttered paper, put on the spit just long enough to warm it, and served just in the same way as roast lamb.

Lamb's head, feet, kidneys, etc., are prepared and served like the same parts of the sheep, and as directed in the different receipts.

KID.

Prepare, cook, and serve kid the same as lamb.

VEAL.

Never buy too young veal. It is very easy to know it; when too young, the bones are very tender; they are more like nerves than bones; the meat is gluish, and has little or no taste. Epicures say that if a calf is killed before it is two months old, or at least six weeks, it is not fit for eating. We are of that opinion, although, perhaps, very few are allowed so long a life. We will therefore recommend our readers to beware buying too young veal; many diseases, especially in children, come from eating it.

When you broil or roast a piece of veal, baste often. Veal is better when a little overdone; it is not good, and operates like physic, if underdone.

The best veal is that of a greenish color and very fat. It is fresh when the eyes are full and smooth, and when the meat is firm. If the meat is yellowish or contains yellowish spots, it is not fresh. The veins must be red.

To improve.—Chop fine a tablespoonful of parsley, a teaspoonful of shallots, same of green onions, a bay-leaf, two sprigs of thyme, two or three mushrooms, add to them, salt, pepper, a little grated nutmeg; cover the bottom of a tureen with half of each, put on it the piece of veal you wish to improve, cover with the other half of the seasonings; then pour gently on the whole two tablespoonfuls of sweet-oil; leave the veal thus about four or five hours in winter and about two in summer.

ROASTED.

The pieces of veal that are roasted are the *loin, leg,* and *shoulder*.

It may be improved as directed above or not, according to taste; but we earnestly recommend it as not a little improvement, but as a marked one, as everybody can try it and judge, veal being naturally tasteless.

There are three ways of roasting veal. We will describe them, so that it can be done according to taste.

1. Spread a thin coat of butter around the piece of veal after being salted all around, put on the spit before a good but not very sharp fire; near it, but not too much so: veal being more tender than beef, it would also burn much quicker. Baste often with melted butter first, and then with the drippings, and from the beginning to the end. When done, that is, when overdone, as veal must always be, serve with the gravy only, or in the different ways described below.

2. Lard all the fleshy parts of the piece of veal with a larding-needle and strips of salt pork, the same as a fillet of beef, but which strips you roll in a mixture of parsley chopped, salt and pepper, before running them into the meat, and proceed as above for the rest. Serve also like the above.

3. After the piece of veal is improved as directed, spread the seasonings in which it has been improved all around it, then envelop the whole in buttered paper, which you fasten with twine, put it on the spit, and baste often with melted butter. It must be basted often to prevent the paper from burning. About fifteen minutes before it is done, remove the paper, put the meat a little nearer the fire so as to give it a fine yellow or golden color, finish the cooking till overdone, and serve also like the first, or No. 1.

No matter which of these three ways the piece of veal is roasted, it is served in the same manner.

With Asparagus.—When the roasted piece of veal is dished, put a *purée* of asparagus all around, and serve warm.

With Peas.—Spread one pint or one quart (according to the size of the piece of meat) of green peas *au jus*, on a dish; place the meat on the peas, spread the gravy over the whole, and serve as warm as possible.

With Quenelles.—Dish the roasted piece, place around it six or eight *quenelles* of chicken or of veal, strain the gravy on the whole, and serve warm.

With Vegetables.—When roasted and dished, put any kind of vegetables, prepared *au jus*, all around the piece of meat, and serve warm.

With Sweetbreads.—Roast the piece of veal as directed, and when dished, place six sweetbreads, prepared *au jus*, tastefully around the meat; strain the gravy over, and serve very warm.

Decorated.—Every piece of roasted veal may be decorated with skewers, either served *au jus* or in any of the above ways. The skewers are first run through either of the following and then stuck into the piece of meat: slices of truffles; chicken-combs, prepared as for garniture; slices of sweetbreads or whole ones, prepared *au jus*; *quenelles* of chicken or of veal; slices of carrots, turnips, beets, all prepared *au jus*; and mushrooms. One, two, three, or more to every skewer; for instance: one slice of truffle, then one of turnip, a chicken-comb, then a slice of sweetbread or a whole one, and then stick in the meat. From two to six skewers may be used. On a large piece never put less than two, and no matter how many you use, always have even numbers of them.

BAKED.

All the parts of veal that are roasted, that is, the loin, leg, and shoulder, can be baked. They may be improved in the same way as to roast them. Put the piece of veal in a bakepan; spread salt, pepper, and butter on it; cover the bottom of the pan with cold water, about a quarter of an inch in depth; place a piece of buttered paper on the meat, and put in a warm oven. If the meat has been improved, the seasonings are spread over it before placing the buttered paper. Baste often with the water and juice in the pan and over the paper, which you need not remove till about ten minutes before taking from the oven, or in case it should burn; then you must replace it by another. It keeps the top of the meat moist, and it is more juicy when done.

When properly baked (overdone, as every piece of veal must be), serve either *au jus*, or with the same garnitures, the same decorations, as directed for roasted veal.

The gravy in the bakepan is strained, the fat skimmed off, and then it is turned over the meat and garnitures when dished, the same as the drippings or gravy of roast meat. In case the water in the bakepan, or the juice, or both, should boil away or be absorbed, put more cold water in it, so as to be able to baste.

BLANQUETTE.—(*Also called Poulette.*)

Take about two pounds of neck, breast, shoulder, or any other piece, which cut in pieces, two inches square, throw them in boiling water, with a little salt, for five minutes, and drain them. Put in a stewpan a piece of butter the size of an egg, set it on a good fire, and when melted mix in a tablespoonful of flour, stirring all the time, and when turning yellow pour gently and slowly in the pan a pint of boiling water; add a teaspoonful of chopped parsley and green onions, salt, pepper, six small white or red onions, two or three mushrooms, and then the meat; boil gently about three hours, and serve.

CROQUETTES.

Proceed as for chicken croquettes in every particular, except that you use cold veal instead of cold chicken.

RAGOUT.

The neck and breast pieces are generally used to make a *ragout*, but any other piece may be used. Take about three pounds of veal, which cut in pieces about two inches square. Put two ounces of butter in a saucepan, set it on the fire, and as soon as the butter is melted, lay the meat in, stir now and then till of a golden color, and then take the meat from the pan. Leave the pan on the fire, and put in it a tablespoonful of flour, little by little, keep stirring about five minutes; add also half a pint of broth, same of warm water, one onion with a clove stuck in it, a bay leaf, two sprigs of thyme, two of parsley, a clove of garlic, a small carrot cut in two or three pieces, salt and pepper, then the meat, and cover the pan. Half an hour after your meat is in, fry in butter in a frying-pan six small onions, which you also put in the stewpan as soon as fried. When the whole is cooked, place the meat on a dish, strain the sauce on it, surround the whole with the six small onions, and serve warm.

In Scallops.—Take a piece from the loin or leg of veal, cut it in pieces about three inches long, two inches broad, and one-third of an inch thick, as evenly as possible, and flatten them with a chopper. Salt and pepper them on both sides, and fry them with a little butter till about half done, on both sides alike. Add a little broth and chopped parsley, and boil gently till done. Place the pieces of veal all around the platter, one lapping over another, turn the sauce in the middle of them, and serve.

Another.—Cut the veal in pieces as for the above; beat one or two eggs in a plate with salt, pepper, and chopped parsley; dip each piece into it and then roll in bread-crumbs; butter a bakepan, place the veal in with a small lump of butter on each piece, and bake; turn over to bake evenly. Serve as the above, with a *piquante* or tomato sauce in the middle.

BREAST, STEWED.

Cut in dice two ounces of bacon, put it in a stewpan and set on a good fire; add two ounces of butter, and two onions cut in slices; when melted, lay the breast in, turn it over and leave till of a golden color on both sides; add then two small carrots cut in pieces, one teaspoonful of chopped green onions, three sprigs of parsley, half a turnip, salt, and pepper; moisten with half a pint of warm water; leave thus about three hours on a moderate fire. Strain the juice in a dish, put the meat on it, and serve.

The pieces of carrots and of bacon may be served with the meat, if you choose.

The same, with Green Peas.—Cut the breast in square pieces about two inches in size. Put in a stewpan a piece of butter the size of an egg, and set it on the fire; when melted, mix in it a teaspoonful of flour, then lay the meat in, and wet with half a glass of broth, same of warm water, also two sprigs of parsley, salt, and pepper; stir now and then. One hour after add green peas, and leave on the fire till the whole is cooked, when skim off the fat on the surface, and serve.

In Matelote.—To make a *matelote* of veal any piece can be used, but most generally it is made with a breast or neck piece. Cut the veal in square pieces about two inches in size; have in a stewpan and on a good fire a piece of butter about the size of an egg; when melted, put the meat in, stir now and then till of a golden color; then take the meat from the stewpan, which you leave on the fire, and in which you put half a pint of warm water, same of claret wine, same of broth, a bay-leaf, two cloves, two sprigs of parsley, one of thyme, a clove of garlic, salt, and pepper; when turning brown, put the meat back in the pan, and fifteen minutes before it is cooked add also ten small onions fried in butter beforehand and four or five mushrooms, then have a brisk fire to finish the cooking; place the meat on a dish, strain the sauce on the meat, put the ten small onions around it, and serve.

Broiled.—Salt and pepper both sides of the breast of veal, grease it all over with melted butter, by means of a brush, and broil till overdone. Serve with a *maître d'hôtel*, *piquante*, or *poivrade* sauce.

CUTLETS.

Broiled.—When properly trimmed, they may be improved as directed for veal. Salt and pepper both sides; spread a little melted butter on both sides also by means of a brush; place them on, before, or under the fire (*see* BROILING); baste now and then with melted butter; turn over one, two, or three times, and when rather overdone serve with a *maître d'hôtel* sauce spread all over.

The above way of serving them is sometimes called *au naturel*.

With Crumbs.—When trimmed, dip them in egg beaten with salt, pepper, and chopped parsley, roll them in bread-crumbs, and then broil and serve them as the above, with a *maître d'hôtel*.

Fines Herbes.—Broil the chops as above, either with or without crumbs, and serve them with sauce *aux fines herbes*.

A l'Italienne.—When broiled as above, serve them on a layer of *macaroni Italienne*.

With Mushrooms.—When broiled and dished, surround them with a garniture of mushrooms, and serve warm. When there are several cutlets on the dish, and placed all around overlapping, the garniture may be put in the middle of the chops.

Do the same with the following garnitures: chicken-combs, *croutons*, *duxelle*, *financière*, *Macédoine*, and onion. They may also be served on any *purée*.

Baked.—Trim six cutlets. Mix well half a pound of sausage-meat with two eggs. Put a piece of buttered paper large enough to cover the bottom of a bakepan in which the six cutlets may be laid easily. Spread half the sausage-meat on the paper in the pan, then lay the cutlets in it; put the other half of the sausage-meat over the cutlets, and place the whole in a rather quick oven. Baste every five minutes with melted butter and broth, using them alternately, and serve warm with the gravy when done. A few drops of lemon-juice may be added to them when on the dish, if liked.

Sautées.—Trim, and fry them with a little butter. When done on both sides, add a little broth, salt, pepper, and mushrooms and parsley chopped fine; chopped truffles may be added, if handy; boil gently for about ten minutes. Place the cutlets around the dish, one lapping over the other, turn the sauce in the middle, sprinkle some lemon-juice over the whole, and serve warm.

With Sauce.—When broiled, baked, or *sautéd*, they may be dished and served with either of the following sauces: *fines herbes*, *maître d'hôtel*, *piquante*, *poivrade*, *ravigote*, *tarragon*, tomato, or truffle.

En Bellevue.—Proceed the same as for fillet of beef *en Bellevue*.

In Papillotes.—Trim six veal-chops, spread salt and pepper on them, and fry them with a little butter till about half done. Take from the fire, and cut a small hole in the middle with a paste-cutter. While they are frying, fry with a little butter one onion chopped fine; as soon as fried, add half a pound of sausage-meat; stir now and then for about five minutes; add also a pinch of cinnamon, same of nutmeg; take off and mix with the whole one yolk of egg, a tablespoonful of chopped parsley, salt, and pepper. Cut six pieces of white paper of a heart-like shape, and large enough to envelop a chop; grease them slightly with butter or sweet-oil; place some sausage-meat on one side of the paper (say half a tablespoonful), place a chop on it; put some sausage-meat on the chop and in the hole; fold the paper in two; then, by folding all around the border, the chop and seasonings are perfectly enveloped in the paper; put the chops in a baking-pan, spread a few drops of oil all over, and bake for about fifteen minutes in an oven at about 250 deg. Fahr. Instead of baking them, broil them carefully turning them over often and basting them to prevent the paper from burning, and serve with the paper on. They may be served on a *duxelle* garniture, or with a *purée*.

Fricandeau.—Take a piece of veal of any size, from the leg, loin, or cutlet piece, about three-quarters of an inch in thickness, lard one side with salt pork, the same as a fillet of beef. Put in a saucepan (for two pounds of meat) one ounce of butter, half a middling-sized onion, and as much carrot in slices, two or three stalks of parsley, one of thyme, a bay-leaf, six or eight pepper-corns, and rind of the pork you have used; spread all these seasonings on the bottom of the saucepan, put the piece of veal on them, the larded side up, set on a good fire for about fifteen minutes; after which you look if the under side of the meat is well browned; if so, add a gill of broth, put in the oven and baste often, if not, leave a little longer on the fire. Add a little broth once in a while, to keep the bottom of the pan wet, and to have enough to baste till a little overdone, and serve with the gravy strained all over it. It is then called *au jus*.

With Spinach.—Prepare and cook the *fricandeau* as above; and when done, put some broth in the pan after having taken off the meat; give one boil; turn in the spinach *au jus*; stir on the fire one minute; dish the spinach; place the *fricandeau* on it, and serve.

With Sorrel.—Proceed as with spinach in every particular, except that you serve on sorrel *au jus* instead of spinach. It makes a more delicate dish with sorrel, although excellent with spinach.

It may also be served with green peas *au jus* or *à l'anglaise*.

Financière.—When prepared, cooked, and dished as directed, surround it with a *financière* garniture, and serve warm.

Jardinière.—After being cooked and dished, put a *Macédoine* garniture around it, and serve warm.

SHOULDER.

Boned.—Lay the shoulder on the table, the inside up, split it just in the middle, lengthwise, and following the middle of the bones; remove the flat bone at the larger end first. Do the same for the remaining bone. Then spread the shoulder open, and salt and pepper it. Fill the inside with sausage-meat; roll it of a round shape, and when properly tied with twine, roast or bake it, as directed for roasted or baked veal. It is then dished, decorated, and served in the same and every way as directed for roasted pieces of veal.

It is an excellent dish served on either of the following purées: *beans*, *celery*, *lentils*, *peas*, *potatoes*, *sorrel*, *spinach*, or *tomatoes*.

When served on a *purée*, it may be decorated with skewers, the same as when served with a garniture.

It may also be served with a *piquante* or *poivrade* sauce.

Stuffed.—Bone the shoulder as directed above; spread it open, and salt and pepper it, also as directed. Spread a coat of sausage-meat on it, about one-third of an inch in thickness, then put a layer of salt pork on the sausage-meat; then a layer of boiled ham; again a layer of sausage-meat; on this a layer of beef or sheep's tongue, boiled. The ham and tongue are cut in square fillets, about one-fourth of an inch broad and about two inches long. The tongues may be fresh or salted, according to taste. When filled, roll it so as to give it a round shape; wrap it up in a towel and drop it in boiling water, to which you have added salt. Boil gently for about four hours, take the kettle from the fire and let cool. When cold take the shoulder off, wipe it dry and serve with meat jelly. The jelly is chopped, or cut in fancy shapes, or both. Some chopped jelly may be placed all around the meat, and some cut in fancy shapes with a paste-cutter or with a knife, and placed over it.

It may also be decorated with skewers, as directed for roasted pieces of veal.

En Bellevue.—When boiled and cold, prepare it like a fillet of *beef en Bellevue*, and serve.

LOIN OR LEG STEWED.

Have in a stewpan and on a slow fire three or four tablespoonfuls of sweet-oil; when hot put the loin in, turn it over till of a yellow color all around, then add a bay-leaf, salt, pepper, and a pint of warm water; simmer four hours, and serve with the following sauce, which you must have prepared at the same time: Fry in butter till of a golden color ten middling-sized onions, then add to them half a glass of claret wine, two tablespoonfuls of broth, and two of the juice of the loin, ten mushrooms (if handy); simmer till cooked, and strain. Mix the sauce with the juice of the loin, and put it on a dish, place the loin upon it, and serve with the onions and mushrooms around the meat.

In case the juice of the loin should be found too fat, throw in it (and before mixing it with the sauce) a few drops of cold water, and skim off the fat.

The only thing to throw away before mixing is the bay-leaf.

Another way, or prepared with a Garniture of Cabbages.—Put in a stewpan and set on a good fire a piece of butter the size of an egg; when melted, add four onions and two small carrots, cut in slices; fry them two or three minutes, then put the loin in, with half a bay-leaf, wet with warm broth; then subdue the fire, let simmer about two hours and a half; strain the sauce on a dish, place the meat on it, and serve with a garniture of cabbages around.

COLD VEAL.

Cut the meat in slices and serve them on a dish, arranged according to fancy, and serve with a *piquante, poivrade, Mayonnaise, Provençale, ravigote,* or *rémolade* sauce. It may also be decorated and served like cold mutton, in *vinaigrette.*

Another way.—Put a piece of butter the size of an egg in a stewpan and set on a good fire, mix in when melted two teaspoonfuls of flour, stir till of a brownish color, when add a saltspoonful of chopped parsley, four leaves of tarragon, salt, pepper, and half a pint of broth (more or less of the above according to the quantity of meat you have left), boil the whole fifteen minutes; then, if what you have left is from an entire piece, cut it in slices, lay them in the pan, and serve when warm enough, as it is.

If what you have left is in pieces or slices, you merely place them in the pan and serve with the sauce when warm.

BRAIN.

To prepare.—Put the brain in a bowl of cold water and a tablespoonful of vinegar and leave it in from one to two or three hours, that is, till you are ready to use it, but do not leave it more than five or six hours and not less than one hour. Take it off, remove the thin skin and blood-vessels that are all around.

To boil.—When prepared, put the brain in a small saucepan, cover it with cold water; add two tablespoonfuls of vinegar, half an onion sliced, three stalks of parsley, one of thyme, a bay-leaf, six pepper-corns, one clove, salt, boil about five minutes and take off the fire. Cut each half of the brain in two, from side to side; place the four pieces on a dish, the part cut upward.

Au Beurre Noir.—When dished as above directed, put two ounces of butter in a frying-pan and when melted turn into it two tablespoonfuls of vinegar, boil two or three minutes, then throw into it half a dozen stalks of parsley, take them off immediately with a skimmer, turn the butter and vinegar over the brain; spread the parsley around, and serve.

Stewed, or in Matelote.—When prepared as directed, put it in a small saucepan and cover it with claret wine; add half an onion sliced, one clove of garlic, one clove, two sprigs of parsley, one of thyme, salt, a bay-leaf, six pepper-corns, and boil gently for about fifteen minutes. Cut and dish it as directed above; turn the sauce over it through a strainer and serve—it is understood, the sauce in which it has been cooked.

Fried.—Prepare as directed, cut in about six slices, dip them in batter, and fry in hot fat. (*See direction for* FRYING.)

In Poulette.—Prepare and boil it as directed, split each half of the brain in two or four pieces, place them tastefully on a dish, spread a *poulette* sauce all over, and serve warm. It may also be prepared and served with a *piquante* sauce. When the *piquante* sauce is made, put the brain or brains in, boil ten minutes, and serve as it is.

EARS.

They are prepared in every way like calf's head.

FEET.

To boil.—Throw them in boiling water for five minutes, split them in the middle and lengthwise after having taken off the large bone and hair, and tie them with a string. Put a piece of butter the size of two walnuts in a stewpan and set it on the fire, when melted add a teaspoonful of chopped parsley and green onions, half of each, a quarter of a lemon cut in slices, salt, and pepper, then the feet; wet with a glass of warm water; boil gently two or three hours, take from the fire and when nearly cold dip them in bread-crumbs, place them on a gridiron and set on a good fire, baste slightly with the juice in which they have cooked, and serve with fried parsley around.

The same, in Poulette.—Prepare and cook them as above. When you take them from the fire, instead of dipping them in bread-crumbs, put them in a *poulette* sauce, simmer ten minutes, and serve.

Fried.—When boiled and drained dry, dip them in beaten egg, roll in bread-crumbs, fry in hot fat, and serve with green parsley all around.

In Vinaigrette.—Boil them as directed and drain them dry. When perfectly cold, serve them with a *vinaigrette*.

CALF'S HEAD.

How to prepare.—When the hair is off and the whole head well cleaned (this is generally done by butchers; but if not, throw the head in boiling water for five minutes and scrape the hair off with a knife immediately after taking it from the water), put it then in cold water for twenty-four hours in winter and ten in summer, changing the water two or three times.

To boil.—It may be boiled whole or after it is boned. If boiled whole, cut a hole on the top of the head and take off the brain without breaking it; put it in cold water immediately and as directed. Then set the head on the fire in a saucepan, covered with cold water, salt, one onion sliced, half a lemon, four stalks of parsley, one of thyme, a bay-leaf, two cloves, two cloves of garlic, ten pepper-corns, and two tablespoonfuls of vinegar; boil gently till done. Bone it before using it.

When boiled after being boned, the brain is taken off in the same way as above and put in cold water also; then the tongue is cut out and boiled with the skin of the head, etc., with the same seasonings as when boiled whole. It is then ready for use, but leave it in the water till wanted; it would become tough if exposed to the air.

In Poulette.—Put about two ounces of butter in a saucepan, set it on the fire, when melted turn in one tablespoonful of flour; stir, and as soon as it commences to turn yellow add half a pint of broth, stir again, and when thickening, add the calf's head cut in rather large dice, give one boil, take from the fire, add the yolk of an egg and about a teaspoonful of chopped parsley, stir, give another boil, and serve.

In Vinaigrette.—Leave it in the water till perfectly cold; or, if wanted immediately, as soon as boiled, take it off and put in cold water to cool, and use. Cut the head in large dice and serve it with oil, vinegar, salt, pepper, mustard, and parsley chopped.

Broiled.—Prepare and boil the calf's head as directed. As soon as cool, cut it in about half a dozen pieces, dip them in beaten eggs, roll them in bread-crumbs, and broil both sides till turning of a golden color; serve warm with a *maître d'hôtel* sauce, or with anchovy or horse-radish butter.

Fried.—Calf's head may be fried as soon as prepared and boiled; but most generally, it is only what has been left from the day before that is fried. Cut it in small pieces about two inches square, dip them in melted butter, roll them in bread-crumbs, and fry them in hot fat. Serve hot, adding lemon-juice when the pieces of calf's head are on the dish.

En Tortue, or Turtle-like.—There are two ways of preparing calf's head en tortue:

1. When it is prepared and boiled as directed above, drain it dry, cut it in pieces as for frying it; put them in a saucepan with one ounce of butter, set on the fire, stir for two minutes, add nearly a pint of Madeira wine, simmer gently for about half an hour; dish the meat, add a little lemon-juice all over, and serve warm. Some *quenelles* of chicken may be placed all around, as a decoration; or a garniture of mushrooms.

2. Prepare and boil the calf's head; drain it dry and cut it in pieces about two inches square. Dish the pieces either mound-like, or around the dish, one lapping over the other, and turn the following over it, and serve warm: Put a *financière* garniture in a saucepan with a pint of Madeira wine, set on the fire and boil gently for about twenty minutes; take from the fire, spread over the pieces of calf's head, and serve.

Some hard-boiled eggs cut in four or eight pieces, lengthwise, may be placed all around the dish; or some pickled cucumbers, cut in fancy pieces, or some quenelles of veal or chicken.

HEART.

To prepare.—Soak it in lukewarm water for about three hours, trim it and free it from skin, blood, and small fibres; then drain and wipe it dry. Stuff or fill it with sausage-meat, to which you add previously two or three onions chopped fine.

To cook.—When thus prepared, envelop it in buttered paper, set on the spit before a good fire, baste often, remove the paper a few minutes before taking it from the fire, then serve warm with a *piquante*, *poivrade*, or *ravigote* sauce. It may also be served with a *vinaigrette*.

To bake.—When prepared as directed above, put it in a baking-pan; spread a little butter over, put a little water in the bakepan and set in a quick oven, baste and turn over two or three times, and when done, serve with the gravy and the same sauces as if it were roasted.

In Gratin.—Soak, drain and wipe it dry as directed.

Cut it in slices and put them in a crockery or other pan; turn a white sauce all over, then sprinkle on half a gill of vinegar or the juice of a lemon, dust with bread-crumbs, put half a dozen lumps of butter, each about the size of a hazelnut, all over; bake in a rather quick oven.

KIDNEYS.

Sauté.—When prepared as directed below, cut it in pieces as directed for kidney in *brochettes*. Then put a piece of butter the size of half an egg in a frying-pan and set it on the fire; when melted, sprinkle in a teaspoonful of flour, stirring with a wooden spoon the while, add half a wine-glass of white wine, a tablespoonful of broth, a pinch of chopped parsley, salt and pepper, boil ten minutes and lay the fillets in; have a quick fire, and as soon as cooked dish them, spread the sauce over, sprinkle on a few drops of lemon-juice, and serve.

To prepare.—Never cook a kidney except it be very fresh. Prepare in the following way, a beef, sheep, or calf's kidney. Pig's kidneys are excellent if they have no disagreeable taste, but it is very often the case. The bad taste may be partly taken away by blanching the kidney, but it makes it tough and tasteless; it is better to throw it away.

In Brochettes.—Split the kidney in four lengthwise, and then cut it in rather small pieces. Cut fat salt pork in pieces of the same size as the pieces of kidney—the fatty part of the kidney must not be used—then salt and pepper the pieces of kidney; take a common skewer and run it through a piece of kidney, then through a piece of salt pork; repeat this till the skewer is full. Fill as many skewers as are necessary till the whole kidney is used; and then roast before a good fire, basting often with melted butter. Serve warm.

Another way.—Prepare as above, and instead of roasting, put the skewers in a bake-pan, spread a little butter over the kidney and salt pork, cover the bottom of the pan only with cold water, and bake. While in the oven, turn over and baste occasionally.

Serve as the above, with its gravy, and warm.

Another.—Skewer the kidney, or rather pieces of kidney and salt pork as above; dip them in beaten egg, roll them in bread-crumbs, and fry them in hot fat. Serve warm, but without gravy.

LIGHTS.

Cut them in four pieces, soak and wash them three or four times in lukewarm water, changing the water each time; press them with the hands to extract all the blood. Place the lights in a stewpan, cover them with cold water, and set on a good fire; boil two minutes, take them off, throw them in cold water, and drain them; cut the lights in dice. Have butter in a stewpan on the fire, and when melted, lay the lights in, fry five minutes, keeping them tossed the while, then sprinkle on a tablespoonful of flour, stirring all the time with a wooden spoon; pour on, little by little, about a pint of warm broth, also a saltspoonful of chopped parsley, a pinch of allspice, salt, pepper, a bay-leaf, and sprig of thyme; have a brisk fire, and when about half done, add four or five mushrooms, and eight small onions. When the whole is cooked, take off bay-leaf and thyme, then take from the fire, beat two yolks of eggs with a tablespoonful of vinegar, and mix with the whole, turn on a dish, and serve.

CALF'S LIVER.

How to prepare.—Have water, with a little salt, on the fire, and at the first boiling, throw the liver in for about five minutes, and drain it.

How to improve the Liver before cooking it.—Put in a tureen two tablespoonfuls of sweet-oil, a bay-leaf broken in four pieces, two sprigs of thyme, four of parsley chopped fine, a green onion also chopped fine, salt, and pepper; lay the liver on the whole, and leave it from four to six hours, turning it over two or three times.

How to cook, roasted.—Envelop the liver with buttered paper, place it on the spit before a good fire, baste often with the oil from the tureen, after having taken off bay-leaf and thyme. A few minutes before it is done, take the paper off, baste continually with the drippings till well cooked, and serve it with the gravy.

It may also be served with a *piquante* or *poivrade* sauce.

It takes from thirty-five to forty-five minutes to roast it.

The same, sauté.—Put two ounces of butter in a frying-pan, and set it on a sharp fire; when melted, add a teaspoonful of chopped parsley and green onions, then the liver cut in slices (after having been prepared as above); sprinkle on a saltspoonful of flour, then half a wine-glass of warm broth, same of claret wine, salt, pepper, and a pinch of allspice; serve when done.

It takes only from ten to twelve minutes for the whole process.

The same, in the Oven.—Put two ounces of butter in a frying-pan on a sharp fire; when hot, put the liver in (after having been boiled as directed above, and after having cut it in pieces); fry it five minutes, turning over once only; then take from the fire, salt both sides of the slices, place them on a warm dish, putting on each slice a little butter kneaded with chopped parsley, salt, and pepper; put two or three minutes in a warm oven, take off, sprinkle on the whole the juice of half a lemon, and serve in the dish in which it has cooked.

www.ingramcontent.com/pod-product-compliance
Lightning Source LLC
Chambersburg PA
CBHW081624100526
44590CB00021B/3596